The 2017 Las Vegas Shooting

The Deadliest Mass Shooting In America,

Inside The Mind And Psychology Of Stephen Paddock

Eric Diaz

TABLE OF CONTENTS

The Las Vegas

Mass Shooting

Nice guy, world traveler, professional gambler

Or…

Reclusive, loner, terrorist.

Who was Stephen Paddock? It seems nobody knew before it was too late and he would commit the deadliest mass shooting in America's history.

The United States has endured many violent acts in its more than 200 years since its founding in 1776, and in the past few decades these violent acts have included mass shootings. A mass shooting is an episode that involves multiple victims being wounded or killed by a firearm or firearms. One popular definition of a mass shooting specifies that the act needs to have at least four victims die by gunfire and the shooting is not related to gang killings, domestic violence, or terrorist acts. However, the exact definition or criteria of what makes a mass shooting is not clear. What is clear, however, is the devastation, destruction, and damage a mass shooting will leave on the lives of its victims and their loved ones.

According to the criteria noted above, one-third of the world's public mass shootings between 1966 and 2012 have occurred on United States soil, and more than 150 mass shootings in America had occurred between 1967 and 2019. From 2007 through 2019 alone, America has suffered from 17 mass shootings, beginning with the Virginia Tech shooting in 2007 and ending with the El Paso Walmart shooting in 2019. In between those two events were some well-known and devastating massacres: the Aurora theater shooting, Sandy Hook Elementary, and the Orlando night club shooting; and some lesser known mass shootings, such as Sutherland Springs church, Santa Fe High School, and Thousand Oaks. However, none of these were as deadly as the 2017 mass shooting in Las Vegas, Nevada, at a three-day country music festival.

No one could have known that on October 1, 2017, the United States would face its deadliest mass shooting in United States history. Yet, on that fateful day, a 64-year-old white man named Stephen Paddock opened fire on around 22,000 attendees of the Route 91 Harvest Music Festival. Paddock killed more innocent victims than any other mass shooting in America's history – he killed 58 individuals, 36 women and 22 men, and injured 869 – 413 specifically injured by gunfire, before killing himself with a gunshot to the head (one additional victim died more than two years later after being paralyzed during the attack).

Thousands of concertgoers would try to flee for safety as Paddock sprayed over 1,000 bullets into the crowd before then taking his own life. More than an hour after his first shot, his body was found by a SWAT team that stormed into his hotel room on the 32nd floor of the Mandalay Bay Hotel and Casino. Not only did they find his lifeless body; Paddock had an arsenal of weapons that could have only been brought up to his hotel room over days on end. At least 23 firearms were found in his hotel room, including a handgun and multiple semi-automatic rifles and AR-15-style assault rifles. Yet, what was even more surprising to those who knew Paddock (beyond him committing the heinous event) was that some of the rifles were equipped with scopes and bump stocks and were accompanied by hundreds of rounds of ammunition. In fact, the investigators would find that the gunman used multiple rifles during his attack. The arsenal he used would also spur legislators and gun activists to bring up the issue of gun control again due to the use of a little-known piece of equipment: something called a bump stock.

By all accounts, Stephen Paddock had a meticulous plan to carry out the deadliest mass shooting in American history – more than 20 guns, thousands of rounds of ammunition, and at least three cameras set up to monitor the corridor outside. He had even requested a high-level, two-room suite overlooking the Route 91 Harvest Festival, but could not immediately get one. This did not deter Paddock, however, from using his time at Mandalay Bay to bring up approximately 10 suitcases filled with firearms and ammunition. So, he stayed in the Mandalay hotel for a few days until, according to a hotel source, he was able to move into the 32nd-floor suite that he used for his attack on Saturday, the night before the mass shooting. He was even given this room for free because the Mandalay Bay Hotel and Casino considered him to be such a good customer, one who gambled tens of thousands of dollars each time he visited the casino.

So again, one may ask, who was Stephen Paddock?

A FAMILIAL CONNECTION?

Stephen Paddock was born in Clinton, Iowa, a small town of nearly 26,000 people that sits along the Mississippi River, to Delores Irene Hudson and Patrick "Benjamin" Paddock on April 9, 1953. Stephen was the eldest of four sons – Stephen, Eric, Bruce, and Patrick. Although Stephen's father and his life that played out like a feature film may not have been known in the history books, it would come to the forefront when Stephen Paddock would commit the most horrific mass shooting in America's history in 2017. Stephen Paddock did not have a criminal record before that night, but he did grow up with a father who was a notorious bank robber who was nicknamed "Big Daddy," "Old Baldy," and "Chromedome" and who became an FBI fugitive throughout the 1960s.

Benjamin Paddock was born in Sheboygan, Wisconsin, on November 1, 1926 to Benjamin Hoskins Paddock Sr. and Olga Emelia Elizabeth Paddock. Benjamin served during World War II as a Seaman Second Class in the Navy and then, in the 1950s, operated a service station in Tucson, Arizona, where he sold used cars. He married Stephen's mom in Reno, Nevada, in 1952, taking on a career selling garbage disposal units for the Arizona Disposer Company. This establishment was also connected to a nightclub in Tucson.

The Paddock family moved from Iowa to Arizona in the 1950s. Benjamin Paddock was known to have held different jobs – he owned his nightclub, worked as a salesman at the Erectrite Corporation, volunteered with the Pima County Juvenile Probation Department, and was even named special deputy to handle cases of wayward youths in 1959. However, Benjamin was not always around during Stephen's early, middle, or later years of life due to his criminal activities.

Benjamin served prison time during the first three years of Stephen's life for stealing a car, participating in a confidence game – a trick that attempts to swindle someone out of money after first gaining their trust – and plotting a scheme to pass bad checks. In 1946, he was convicted of 10 counts of auto larceny and five counts of confidence game and was detained at the Illinois State Penitentiary until July 1951. He was convicted of conspiracy due to his connection to a bad check passing operation, returning to the Illinois State Penitentiary. Stephen's father was released from prison in August 1956 and the family then moved to Arizona.

Although it may have looked like the Paddocks were going to start fresh in a new state, this is where things got worse. In February 1959, Benjamin was accused of robbing $11,210 from branches of the Valley National Bank of Arizona. More than a year later, in July 1960, he would again be accused of robbing another branch for $4,620. Benjamin would also be arrested in 1960 for bank robbery in Las Vegas (although he was living in Tucson, Arizona, with his family) when Stephen was only seven years old. He was arrested and convicted of third robbery in federal court in January 1961.

Labeled by the FBI as "a glib, smooth-talking con man," Benjamin even tried to run down an FBI agent with his car during the Las Vegas pursuit. The elder Paddock would be sentenced to 20 years in prison. Agents had even searched the family's Arizona home for evidence, during which a neighbor,

Eva Price, took the young Stephen swimming. Benjamin Paddock was accused of stealing around $25,000 from three bank branches in Arizona, yet he would escape from prison six months after his sentencing.

On December 30, 1968, Benjamin Paddock escaped from the Federal Correctional Institution, La Tuna, in Anthony, Texas. A warrant for his arrest would be issued on February 3, 1969, earning Benjamin Paddock a spot on the FBI's Most-Wanted Fugitives List from June 10, 1969 until May 5, 1977. Most individuals who are placed on the FBI's "Ten Most Wanted" list are usually only on it for about six months – Benjamin Paddock was on this list for eight years. In fact, after the elder Paddock escaped from La Tuna federal prison, an FBI wanted poster from 1969 described the him as an avid bridge player and stated that: "Paddock diagnosed as psychopathic, has carried firearms in commission of bank robberies," and "He reportedly has suicidal tendencies and should be considered armed and very dangerous."

At the time, Benjamin was over six feet tall, nearly 250 pounds, and had a scar above his right eye brow and on his right knee. He was a smooth talker who liked smoking cigars and cigarettes, eating steaks, and, of course, enjoyed gambling (a possible precursor to his son's "job" years later). Benjamin also went under numerous aliases – "Perry Archer," "Benjamin J. Butler," "Leo Genstein," and "Pat Paddock," and was on the run until September 6, 1978 when he was arrested at a bingo parlor he operated in Springfield, Oregon, under the alias "Bruce Warner Ericksen." While living in Oregon, he would work as a contract trucker and in drug abuse rehabilitation before applying for a license to open his bingo parlor. He was even operating his bingo parlor for a non-profit organization called the Center for Education Reform, a group based in Eugene. However, "Bruce" could not give up Benjamin's criminal tendencies, and in 1978 he was arrested and later released on parole. Nearly a decade later, in 1987, the Oregon Attorney General charged Benjamin with racketeering related to his bingo parlor and fraud for illegally rolling back automobile odometers. This time, he would avoid prison time and just be hit with a $100,000 fine. Benjamin Paddock pleaded no contest to the charges and did not receive any jail time. During his later years, Benjamin Paddock lived quietly in Texas where he owned a car shop with his girlfriend, dying on January 18, 1998 in Arlington, Texas, at the age of 71.

Stephen Paddock's mother would move her children to Southern California as a single mother who pretended her criminal husband was dead (as he continued to break the law without the shadows of his family). Stephen's mother had told her sons that their father had died, even though at that time he was serving time in prison. She worked as a secretary and tried to raise her boys on her own the best she could. In the meantime, while Stephen's mother was taking care of her kids alone, his father was paroled in 1979 and returned to his bingo operation in Oregon and continued to run scams, including claiming to be a pastor of a nondenominational church. According to family members, Stephen had limited contact with his father and was basically raised by a single mother. Stephen's younger brother, Eric, explained that Stephen and his brothers really did not know their father well at all and, by all accounts: "We didn't grow up under his influence." Eric Paddock explained. Eric was born when the family was literally on the run in Tuscon and his father was about to be arrested for bank robbery.

LIKE FATHER, LIKE SON?

Benjamin Paddock was labeled a psychopath, but does that mean that his son, Stephen, also could have been one? Psychopathy is heritable, and the fact that Stephen Paddock was divorced twice was a characteristic of a psychopath – broken relationships. However, there was not much data to back up a heritable trait of psychopathy just because Stephen Paddock's father was called one. Donald Judy, a former next-door neighbor, said about Paddock that "He was always normal" and Stephen's younger brother, Eric, broke down into tears when he found out and said, "We are completely dumbfounded." No one saw the terrors of Benjamin Paddock as a prelude to what Stephen Paddock would do on October 1st in Las Vegas, not even Stephen's brother, Eric.

Eric knew his older brother owned firearms, and even had his children go skeet shooting with their uncle, but besides that there was nothing out of the blue about his brother and firearms. The last time Eric spoke with his older brother, Stephen had texted him to ask how their 90-year-old mother was doing. This was certainly not out of the ordinary – it was mid-September and Hurricane Irma had swept through their mother's Orlando, Florida, neighborhood and cut the power. This was the same older brother who sent boxes of cookies to their mom, played $100 poker hands, ate burritos from Taco Bell, and went on cruises. Two weeks after that text, Eric's older brother would be found dead by a self-inflicted gunshot wound after he opened fire on a country music festival.

"Something just incredibly wrong happened to my brother."

But who really was Stephen Paddock? Was he mentally affected by his father's criminal life and psychopathic mental issues? To those who knew him, 64-year-old retiree Stephen Paddock did not seem like the typical mass shooter – to his family and friends, he was simply a former real estate investor and property manager and was an avid gambler. He had no criminal history on federal, state, or local records and did not have any derogatory information on background checks, which were required to purchase firearms. Stephen Paddock also reportedly had no religious or political affiliations. Paddock's girlfriend, Marliou Dandy, who was Catholic, explained that Stephen was an atheist who would blame her if she made a sign of the cross and then something negative happened afterward, a typical post hoc fallacy. He was not known to discuss politics, race, or gun control, and he did not belong to political organizations.

Even though Paddock was not affiliated with any religious or political organizations, it would later be remarked by those who knew him that Stephen Paddock was vocal of his support for President Donald Trump and many of the president's policies. For one, he was interested in the president's politics because of the improvement in the stock market after Trump took office; stocks had risen virtually every month after Trump took office. Paddock was also known to comment on his belief that Trump would stop illegal immigration. But those views alone were not a warning sign of the mass killing at a country music festival.

In addition, Stephen Paddock did not show signs of mental illness. In fact, most people with mental illness are not violent and are actually victims of violent crimes rather than the perpetrator of one. Paddock also was not known to have an unhealthy interest in guns. He was never seen at any local gun clubs or shooting ranges. By all accounts he was an upstanding citizen – he was university educated and had worked as an accountant, an auditor, an apartment manager, and was a licensed pilot who owned two planes, obtaining the license on November 17, 2003 and allowing him to fly a single-engine and instrument airplane. Records also showed he needed to wear glasses when flying for what was called "near vision." In addition, Paddock obtained fishing licenses from Alaska.

Stephen Paddock had lived a pretty successful life as a lucrative real estate investor. He spent much of his life living in the Greater Los Angeles area from the 1970s to the early 2000s and owned personal property in Panorama City, Cerritos, and North Hollywood, as well as co-owning two apartment buildings in the working-class neighborhood of Hawthorne, California and an apartment complex in the Dallas suburb of Mesquite, Texas. Paddock purchased the 111-unit apartment complex in Mesquite for $8.4 million, using some of the profits from selling smaller properties in Los Angeles – the mortgage of $3.5 million and $4.9 million were largely in proceeds from the California real estate. He was even known to run the complex as a manager and accountant, living on the property in order to keep his expenses at a minimum. Residents remembered him roaming around the property making causal conversations with them. When he sold the apartments a decade later, it was reported that he probably profited between $5 million to $6 million from the sale.

During this time, his former brother-in-law, Scott Brunoehler (whose sister, Sharon, married Stephen in 1977), remembered Stephen being fun and smart, entertaining on his boat and, according to Brunoehler, literally "seemed like a normal, good guy." Stephen was even described as liking country music, a juxtaposition to his actions during the Route 91 Harvest

Country Music Festival. Why would someone with an affinity to country music target an event that had individuals who had the same musical interest?

Stephen Paddock had no formal military background, and by all accounts no one would have thought he would be acclimated to use firearms, moreover weapons that worked similarly to automatic weapons. He was said to be worth at least $2 million in his real estate business ventures and was not a social media user and did not maintain a Facebook or Twitter page. But again, being invisible on social media did not make for a killer, as his brother, Eric, noted when interviewed about the massacre: "Is he such a weirdo because he didn't have a Facebook page and posted 50,000 damn pictures of himself every day? Who's weird?"

Paddock eventually sold his two-bedroom home in Florida for $235,000, taking an $11,000 hit, yet his brother Eric had touted Stephen's wealth and said that he made approximately $2 million when the brothers sold off a real estate business they were running together. Stephen also profited immensely when he sold an apartment building he had owned with his former wife and other family members for $3.2 million in 2004. According to Eric, his brother was a multi-millionaire who also made him wealthy. He even told reporters after his brother committed the worst mass shooting in United States history that they were wealthy and an amount like $100,000 was not that much money to Stephen. According to those who knew him and those who worked at the casinos he had frequented, Paddock had gambled that much through a machine in hours. In addition, Eric made an interesting claim about the hotels themselves that may have distanced themselves from Paddock after the mass shooting: "He's got the highest level of membership card at a lot of these [casino] hotels. If a lot of these hotels say they don't know Steve, they're lying."

Together, the brothers saved money from their day jobs to put a down payment on real estate, and this was just a small portion of the real estate options owned by Stephen Paddock. Eric remembers a time when the entire family took over the top floor of the Atlantis in Reno at the casino's expense. Eric also recalled even bringing his son, who was in his 20s, to visit Stephen and spend a weekend at the Wynn Las Vegas hotel and casino, where the elder Paddock had achieved "Chairman's Club" status. A casino employee at the Wynn was assigned to service Paddock for six years, during which the gambler made more than 100 trips to the casino. He had described Paddock as the perfect customer – he never lost his temper, always paid his debts, and never complained when he was losing. Eric even remembers his brother taking his son skeet-shooting – paid for by a casino – and also ordering them a sushi meal that had to be worth $1,000, but was also fully comped by the casino.

Paddock then moved with his girlfriend to an upscale and quiet retirement community in 2015 called Sun City in Mesquite, Nevada, that seemed more like an oasis than a retirement community. At one point in time, Paddock and Hadley were living in at least three different retirement communities. However, Sun City was an exclusive community about 80 miles north of Las Vegas for residents aged 55 and older. The area had, among other amenities, outdoor swimming pools and an 18-hole golf course. Paddock could relax, play golf, and travel a little over an hour from his home to his second home: the casinos. He bought the 2,018-square foot home for $369,022, only two years after already purchasing a $238,000 home in 2013 in the Reno area of Sierra Canyon by Del Webb community. He sold the Reno home in 2016.

Stephen Paddock and his girlfriend had lived in Sun City for nearly a year, but not many other residents knew him. He would stay in casino hotels for months at a. When he was home in Sun City, Paddock seemed to keep to himself, so the neighbors were obviously horrified when they found out their community was the home of a killer. With a population of around 18,000 full-time residents and 20,000seasonal residents, for several years the town of Mesquite had even ranked as one of Nevada's safest cities. And many retirees found the area attractive because they could live in year-round sunshine with no state income tax. Although Paddock was not the most sociable resident, this was not uncommon in the town of Mesquite that boded a large population of both retirees and seasonal residents who do not get too involved in activities.

When authorities searched his light-orange, single-story stucco Mesquite home in the Sun City community, nothing unusual was found, with Quinn Averett, a Mesquite police officer, quoted as stating that it was a "nice, clean home and nothing out of the ordinary." However, Paddock had a large safe of guns in his garage, and after the massacre officers found a stockpile of weapons and ammunition during their search of his two homes in Nevada.

Paddock had lived a transient life that took him from area to area without settling down for long periods of time – in total, he had 27 different residences in Texas, California, Florida, and Nevada. Paddock had originally lived in Texas and California before moving near his mother and brother in Melborne, Florida, for several years. He would tell his Florida neighbors, however, that he lived in Las Vegas but wanted a place in Florida so he could search for a home for his mother. His Florida neighbor, Don Judy, remembers Paddock's home looking more like a dorm room than a home of a grown man. There was no art on the walls, no car in the driveway, no furniture for entertaining. Instead, Paddock's residence consisted of a dining chair, two recliners, and a bed. Judy also remembers his wife being shown a laptop by Paddock that showed he had just won $20,000 just from betting online. More recently, Paddock had purchased a walker for his 90-year-old mother and had it shipped from Nevada to Florida. Certainly not a portrait of a mass killer, but he was one nonetheless but, instead, a wealthy retiree who turned in his real estate hat for a gambling one. However, the massive funds Stephen Paddock had accumulated over his life helped him do two things – he was able to support his high-stakes gambling and he was able to buy tens of thousands of dollars' worth of rifles, bullets, and equipment to commit the massive attack in Las Vegas.

A UNIVERSITY-
EDUCATED MASS SHOOTER

S tephen Paddock's educational resume also does not paint a picture of a mass killer. He graduated from the Los Angeles Unified School District Schools, attending Richard E. Byrd Middle School in 1965, John H. Francis Polytechnic High School, graduating in 1971, and California State University, Northridge, graduating in 1977, in which he attained a degree in business administration. Friends from both middle and high school were understandably shocked when they saw Paddock's familiar face all over the news in connection with the mass shooting. Former Los Angeles City Councilman Richard Alarcon, for example, played baseball and football with Paddock and attended John Francis Polytechnic High with him in which they both graduated in 1971. Stephen Paddock was known as a smart kid in high school, dressing like a hippie and rebelling the geek stereotype of other smart high schoolers. Although they were not close friends, Alarcon recognized his face and said, if he had to pick someone to commit this horrific crime, Paddock would have been among the last. Basically, Paddock was an average, American kid, according to Alarcon.

Cal State Northridge is noted as a diverse university, spreading across a 356-acre campus in Los Angeles' San Fernando Valley and educating nearly

40,000 students by more than 4,000 faculty and staff members. When current Cal State Northridge students heard that one of their alumni carried out the deadly crime in Las Vegas, they were shocked, stunned, horrified, and saddened that the shooter graduated from their university. The Cal State Northridge Chief of Police, Anne Glavin, learned of the news at 4 a.m. on Monday, and immediately began conducting due diligence – sending out a written statement of condolences to the victims, survivors, first responders and loved ones, and gathering any and all records about Paddock as a student at Cal State Northridge – before the news spread across the campus. The Cal State Northridge police were contacted and university officials shared information with Las Vegas investigators.

After college, Stephen Paddock worked for the United States Postal Service as a letter carrier from 1976 through 1978 and then as an agent for the Internal Revenue Service from 1978 through 1984. Other significant careers followed – he was a Defense Contract Audit Agency auditor in 1984 and 1985 and then an internal auditor for three years for a company that would later be the defense contractor Lockheed Martin.

A DIVORCED AND
UNFRIENDLY PERSONAL LIFE

Stephen Paddock was married two times and never had any children. This first marriage to Sharon Brunoehler only lasted a few years, from 1977 to 1979, and his second marriage was from 1985 through 1990 to a woman named Peggy Okamoto. The couple divorced due to irreconcilable differences. With no wife and no children – and lots of money – Paddock took up the hobby-turned-career of gambling. He was a retiree with time on his hands and no one to hold him back, so gambling would quickly turn into a job for him where he would make an adequate nest egg.

During the time of the massacre, Paddock was living with his girlfriend, 62-year-old Marilou Danley, a proud mother and grandmother according to her Facebook page. The couple met when Danley worked at the Atlantis Casino Resort and Spa in Reno, Nevada's third-largest city and a popular gambling destination. Danley's job was to enroll gamblers for frequent-customer cards before then becoming a high-limit hostess for Club Paradise, a rewards program at the hotel. Paddock was not the most liked patron at the Atlantis; for example, he would often move to a gambling machine when someone who was using it simply got up to take a break. He was also known to light up cigars when someone would sit beside him, aiming the smoke right into the patron's face even though he did not even smoke. Although this would anger his fellow patrons, Paddock did not seem to care – the machines were for him. He was also known to stare at other people playing, which would make other high rollers and VIPs in the high-limit area very uncomfortable. It was almost like he was silently challenging them to a staring contest, and according to one guest, this type of behavior made this person respond that: "He really gives me the creeps." But there was an attraction between he and Danley.

Danley was married at the time of their meeting but left her husband in 2013 to move in with Paddock. She officially divorced her husband, Geary Danley, in 2015 after 25 years of marriage. In August 2017 a little over a month before the shooting, Paddock purchased a vehicle with a $14,411 check and, during the test drive, told a sales woman at a Reno car dealership that he had saved Danley from a troubled marriage. She was a citizen of Australia (although born in the Philippines) and had a daughter from a previous relationship who lived in Los Angeles.

The couple was not antisocial during their time together and Danley was known by casino patrons to constantly be by Paddock's side. Nearly every week the couple frequented a local Mesquite establishment and popular bar in town, Peggy Sue's Bar and Diner, where they would sing karaoke while having some drinks. The couple were regulars at Friday night karaoke where Danley liked to sing. They would also stay in the most extravagant accommodations in Reno, California, and Las Vegas, courtesy of Paddock and his winnings. According to Stephen's brother, Eric, "They were adorable — big man, tiny woman. He loved her. He doted on her."

Danley was also very sympathetic to Stephen's quirks, particularly his germ and allergy fears. Paddock was very vocal about being sick and sensitive from chemical smells, and Danley changed her way of life to accomodate these complaints. For example, Paddock often wore gloves to prevent rashes from contacting cleaning chemicals and wanted his girlfriend to not wear perfumes or hairspray. These peculiarities were illustrated in a picture that circulated in the media of Danley after Paddock committed the mass shooting. According to Eric, "The reason Mary Lou [sic] looks so plain in that picture they keep posting of her is because for him she would not wear perfumes or hair sprays or anything with scents in it because it affected him." Eric texted this message to the media once a picture of Danley started circulating and showing her to be plain, with no makeup.

Danley empathized with the fact that Paddock was germaphobic and strongly reactive to smells. In fact, he was not able to renew his pilot's license because he was allergic to the pills he needed to take to reduce his blood pressure to keep the license. In addition, the casinos in which he was a regular also accommodated his requests that they wash his room's carpet with plain water to further avoid chemicals. Investigators of the mass shooting thought Paddock's obsession with cleanliness could have been a sign of bipolar disorder (although this disorder could not be identified in the post-mortem examination of Paddock's brain after his apparent suicide by gunshot). A primary care physician who also believed Paddock may have been inflicted with bipolar disorder said he did not want to talk about it and only took anxiety medication, not antidepressants. Paddock was known to be fearful of medication and often refused to take it even when needed. The doctor also described Paddock's behavior as odd and as a man who showed very little emotion.

This lack of emotion could have just been nervousness of being at the doctor or being an introvert. Or, studies have shown it could also be a medical condition known as alexithymia. This mostly unknown medical condition is the inability to identify and describe the emotions one experiences either by oneself or with others. Some signs of alexithymia include having problems

20

with social attachments, with interpersonal relating, and with one's own emotional awareness. Did Stephen Paddock have this ailment? After Stephen's death, psychologists did see some clear similarities between Paddock's mannerisms and those suffering from alexithymia, but there is not clear answer. Yet, one in 10 people do suffer from alexithymia, so it could have been a common ailment even Stephen Paddock did not know of or learn about until it was too late.

Sun City residents saw a stark contrast in the demeanors of Stephen Paddock and Marilou Danley. Neighbors of the couple saw Danley as a happy, friendly woman who gardened in their front yard, waved hello to passersby, and took Zumba classes in the community clubhouse. However, neighbors described Paddock as standoffish, weird, reclusive, and unfriendly. Besides possibly seeing him when he worked out at the community clubhouse, Paddock kept to himself and did not socialize with those living in the community. One neighbor even noted that Stephen Paddock would keep to himself and how "it was like living next to nothing."

Not everyone was very complimentary of the couple. For example, Esperanza Mendoza, a supervisor at a Starbucks in Reno's Virgin River Casino that the couple frequented, told the *Los Angeles Times* that Stephen Paddock would criticize Danley frequently and was very rude to her in front of the employees and patrons. Another individual said to be their neighbor noted that she did have pleasant conversations with Danley, but that Paddock was aggressively unfriendly. Most of the time, Paddock and Danley kept their blinds closed, but once in a while Paddock would open his garage door and some neighbors then saw he had a large safe the size of a refrigerator in his garage. Yet, his brother, Eric, explained that someone who keeps the blinds closed is not weird. Instead, he said his brother was simply a private man.

Another friend did note that Paddock showed him that he had a "gun room" at his Mesquite, Nevada, home and that Paddock explained that it is one of his hobbies that needs protecting. Paddock had studied arguments supporting his Second Amendment rights under the United States Constitution. When he discussed gun laws, Paddock's knowledge on the right to bear arms was exceptional compared to the average defender of the Second Amendment. However, he did not take the man inside the room or show off his collection of weapons. What could have been seen as odd, however, was the fact that Paddock erected a mesh privacy screen around his Mesquite property and was later forced to take it down after his neighbors signed a petition. But, a need for privacy still was not a sign of a mass murder to those living around him.

After the Las Vegas shooting, Danley was adamant that there were no signs that her boyfriend would commit such a brutal massacre and would make an official statement, read by her attorney in front of the FBI's Los Angeles office, that she did not have any advanced warning of the attack. "He never said anything to me or took any action that I was aware of that I understood in any way to be a warning that something horrible like this was going to happen," Danley said in a statement printed in *The New York Times*. She would have no explanation for her boyfriend's horrific actions and only knew him as kind, caring and quiet – certainly not the profile of a mass killer.

Luckily, Danley was out of the country when her boyfriend killed nearly 60 innocent victims and injured hundreds. Her sisters said she was sent away by Paddock to the Philippines so that she would not interfere with his murderous plans. According to Danley, Stephen had told her he found a cheap ticket for her to fly to the Philippines. Then, he wired her $100,000 to a Philippines account and told her to buy a house for herself and her family there before the massacre. It was initially his idea for her to take a trip home to visit her family, and she had initially thought the trip and the wired money was Paddock's way of breaking up with her. She had even told investigators that he had grown more distant over the year before the shooting.

Danley arrived in the Philippines on September 15 before leaving on September 22, returning to the Philippines three days later on a flight from Hong Kong. So, Danley was in Asia at the time of the shooting and did not arrive back in the United States from the Philippines until after the massacre had occurred. Although she would end up being a person of interest, she would not be charged with any crimes.

MASS SHOOTER
OR HIGH ROLLER? OR BOTH?

Unlike other mass shooters of the past, Stephen Paddock gave no inkling to family, friends, or social media correspondences of his deadly intentions. By all accounts, he was an average 64-year-old man – no prior run-ins with the law, no arrests, only a minor traffic citation in Las Vegas years before the massacre that he settled out of court. "He's never even drawn his gun before…He was a guy. He gambled," said his brother, Eric. Eric knew of five guns his brother owned and kept locked in a safe, but he was stunned when he heard Stephen used a rapid-fire weapon, similar to an automatic rifle, in the Las Vegas shooting. He also was not aware that his brother had any form of mental illness, alcohol or drug problems, anything that could have been an indication as to why he snapped and did such a horrific crime.

Stephen Paddock only fits one stereotype of the typical mass shooter – he was male and he was white. This stereotype has been perpetuated for decades; a white male with a history of either mental illness or domestic violence goes on a killing spree in a highly-populated area. And, white males do own more guns in the United States than any other group. How many people own guns in the United States? There are more than one billion small arms issued globally and more than 800 million of them are owned by civilians. As for the United States, around 46 percent of those numbers are owned by American civilians. That means around 30% of American adults are gun owners and, among them, two-thirds own more than one firearm and 29% of them own more than five guns.

The demographic of gun owners in the United States does match the demographic of what the stereotype is of a mass shooter – white males. Nearly half, 48%, of gun owners are in fact white males, compare to only 24 percent%of nonwhite men and white women. Yet, recent history has shown that race does not play a single factor in whether someone will commit a mass shooting.

If one researches other recent mass shootings, this stereotype of mass shooters being both male and white may not hold water. The mass shooting with the second highest deaths in America, the Orlando nightclub shooting in June 2016, was carried out by a 29-year-old security guard named Omar Mateen who, although male, was of Afghanistan decent. Both of his parents were from Afghanistan and it was said by survivors of his mass shooting, which killed 49 people, that he was vocal about trying to spare black people (which may have meant he was intent on killing white people). According to a survivor of the Orlando shooting, Mateen asked if there were any black people in the bathroom in which she was hiding during the nightclub massacre and then the killer stated that "I don't have a problem with black people…this is about my country. You guys suffered enough." Mateen was shot and killed by police and, up until Stephen Paddock, had committed the worst mass shooting in American history.

The next largest mass shooting was committed on April 16, 2007 at Virginia Tech by Seung-Hui Cho, an undergraduate student of South Korean origin whose family immigrated to the United States when Cho was eight years old. Cho was diagnosed in middle school with selective mutism, which is a severe form of anxiety disorder, along with a major depressive disorder. These issues that Cho faced brought up the subject of mental illness and firearms after he committed his horrific mass shooting in Virginia. Cho shot and killed 32 people and injured 17 others with two semi-automatic weapons (the deadliest mass shooting until Mateen and, later, Paddock). Cho committed suicide by shooting himself in the head.

That being said, gender, race, and mental stability are not the most common traits of mass shooters. Mass shootings have long been a powerfully partisan debate – many liberals blame guns while many conservatives blame mental health. However, both sides may be correct. A mass shooting is the killing of four or more people in a public place, and mass shooters have consistently had four things in common: childhood trauma, a personal crisis or specific grievance, other examples that give their own feelings validation, and access to firearms. Based on all accounts, Stephen Paddock only had the fourth, access to firearms.

Access to firearms is not surprising; a recent study found that, although younger school shooters usually obtained their guns from family or friends, more than half of all mass shooters studied obtained their guns illegally. But what is surprising about Paddock was, unlike many of the mass shooters in recent history, he was apparently not motivated by religious, racist, or misogynist views. For example, the United States has suffered shootings that targeted black churchgoers in Charleston, South Carolina, Jews at a synagogue in Pittsburgh, women at a yoga studio in Tallahassee, Florida, and Latinos at a Walmart in El Paso, Texas. These shootings all have one thing in common: hate toward a specific group. However, the only group Paddock really targeted was country music lovers, yet he was also known to listen to country music. In addition, although he was the son of an outlaw, his father's criminal past did not seem to leave any childhood trauma or scars.

Paddock also did not fit the mass shooter profile of individuals who kill in a commercial location. This is one of five profiles of mass shooters: elementary, secondary, high school shooters; college and university shooters; workplace shooters; places of worship shooters; and the one that Paddock fits in best – shooters at a commercial location. Paddock was older than that profile, which is usually a white male in his 30s. And many of these shooters have either a violent history or criminal record, yet Paddock had neither. In addition, these types of shooters usually use a single, legally obtained firearm (for example, in a restaurant, mall, or store), but Paddock had an arsenal of weapons for his much larger location. In fact, handguns were found to be more common and used three times the rate of the shotguns, rifles, and assault rifles that Paddock used,. Many times, these shooters are also inflicted with thought disorders, such as schizophrenia, paranoia, or delusions, yet Paddock seemed to only suffer from anxiety. Finally, the same study found a compelling link between suicidal motivations and mass shootings, but investigators of the Las Vegas shooting were convinced Paddock had planned on escaping after his massacre was complete. It seemed he only killed himself when he realized there was no way out.

Stephen Paddock's motive, or lack thereof, also became a point of contention in the investigation of the Las Vegas mass shooting. When one researches past mass shootings, the motive of the killer is usually clear. For example, when Nidal Hassan shot and killed 13 people at Fort Hood in Texas in 2009, authorities had known that Hassan had reached out to radical clerics in the Middle East. Similarly, when Omar Mateen killed 49 people at the Pulse Nightclub in Orlando, Florida, he confessed in a phone call to police that he was a sympathizer of the Islamic State of Iraq and Syria (ISIS). Less than a year later, in December 2016, Dylann Roof walked into a Columbia, South Carolina, church and killed nine people after confessing to his friends of his intention to kill and posting a white supremacy manifesto online.

However, this was not the case with Stephen Paddock. Did he have financial troubles from years of gambling? Was he having relationship issues with his girlfriend? Was he abusing drugs or alcohol? Did an act of terrorism, political, or religious views fuel his hate? There were no signs in Stephen Paddock's life to explain why he meticulously planned the mass shooting in Las Vegas. He had no connections to any extremist groups, left no known manifesto, and shared his plans with no one. Although he was an avid gambler, Paddock did not owe anyone large amounts of money and was known to pay off any gambling debts he had. His actions were a true mystery.

Paddock was a wealthy retiree who seemed to have made most of his riches from real estate sales and gambling winnings. In fact, those who knew him had assumed he was a profitable gambler based on his bets, his travels, and his Vegas lifestyle. Stephen Paddock was known in certain circles to be rather wealthy, which is uncommon when one researches the profile of a mass shooter. In fact, research has shown that many mass shooters, who are mostly white males, perform their violence to regain status they may have lost through a powerful act that shapes their masculinity. It was well known that Stephen Paddock was an avid gambler, both online and in the casinos themselves, and his wealth placed him well above the average middle class. He even referred to himself as a professional gambler, and in addition to owning numerous homes for both pleasure and real estate, Stephen applied for a passport in 2010 and went on 20 cruises to Spain, Greece, Italy, Jordan, and the United Arab Emirates, to name a few. And, of course, many of the cruise ships had casinos on board. His girlfriend, Marilou Danley, accompanied Paddock on nine of those cruises and he was considered by many to be a very generous man whenever he and Danley were with other couples. The couple would essentially leave their homes vacant for months on end to stay at various casinos, travel on cruises and to different places using millions of free airline miles and enjoy the life of a professional gambler.

Paddock preferred to stay in casino hotels rather than the homes he owned, sometimes living the hotel life for weeks on end in order to "work" the gambling machines.

In addition to his Reno home, Paddock bought a newly constructed two story house on Babbling Brook Court in Mesquite with Danley, and he noted on the application that his income came from gambling. He even told the real estate agent that he gambled about $1 million a year. This made Paddock much richer than the other mass shooters throughout history (in addition to being older than many of the other white males who committed mass shootings). He spent a lot gambling and enjoyed the perks, from free stays in the top hotel suites to even winning a car. He was a top gambler in the city and was known in gambling circles as a high roller who would sit in front of slot machines and video poker for hours upon hours. These were the machines that did not draw attention; a person could sit in front of them for hours, wagering as much as they would like, and no one would think it was odd. The casino hosts did know him well, and he would play several hundred hands an hour.

Stephen Paddock did not look like an average high-rolling gambler, let alone a mass shooter. Yet, he was attracted to the high-dollar machines that were separated from the average players and relied on mathematical strategy versus emotional choices. Paddock did not worry about the poker tables nor did he frequent them with his gambling funds; he only used his mathematical algorithms on the video poker machines.

A WELL-KNOWN
VIDEO POKER GAMBLER

Hotel staff at the Mandalay Bay Hotel and Casino had noted that Paddock visited their site about twice a month, and he was even seen playing video poker at the Mandalay Bay Hotel and Casino three days before the horrific massacre. Unlike the everyday gambler, Paddock would play video poker machines located in a separate area of the Mandalay Bay. This quiet room was "High Limit Slots" and had its own attendants and cocktail waitresses who were more attentive to the players' needs and restrooms to keep the high rollers from leaving the area. This was the full-service gambling Paddock enjoyed; no waiting to cash tickets, no waiting for machines, no waiting for drinks. Many of the seats in these high-end areas were adjustable so that the gambler had the perfect, most comfortable gambling experience. So, players will spend hours upon hours gambling in these sectioned-off settings away from others.

Paddock was known to gamble after dark and sleep during the day, and was spotted at times in the high-limit rooms when in the casinos, yet his game of choice was video poker – he had played those machines enthusiastically for more than 25 years. He even described himself, in his own words in a 2013 court deposition, as the "biggest video poker player in the world" who averaged 14 hours a day, every day. Video poker, also called the "crack cocaine of gambling," began in the 1970s when a man named William Reed merged gambling with video game technology. By 1980, Reed had founded the International Game Technology and would become known as the "King of Video Poker." Reed's video poker idea was a success because, on one hand, it allowed amateur players who may have been intimidated to play poker with live people to still enjoy the game. On the other hand, the machines ended up becoming very addicting to players who end up getting hooked on the game like drugs. How does a game do this? It coerces the players to keep playing with the hopes that the next hand with be their big win.

Video poker may receive less attention than the poker played at the tables with actual people, especially with the famous "World Series of Poker" tournaments placing the game into the spotlight. Since the video poker player is not playing against real opponents, there is no bluffing or agonizing about what the other players have in their hand. Video poker machines also do not make human errors or distract the players with mannerisms. It was about the cards on the video screen, and players like Paddock could play 10 hands in a minute since each hand requires only a few second of time for experts like Paddock.

There is no emotion, no intuitions about other players, no camaraderie – video poker is a lonely game of using mathematics to calculate odds. And, lonely they are, video poker machines do not usually attract tourists interested in the excitement of playing poker with others and a real-life dealer. Instead, these machines were more for the locals who were there for one thing: making money. According to his brother, Eric, Stephen Paddock did not visit casinos for fun; instead, he viewed casinos as a job, a means to an end. To those that knew him well, Stephen Paddock was intelligent and methodical while also being guarded and calculated. But Eric also remembered his brother as generous, someone who used his gambling winnings to take care of his family as well as live a lavish lifestyle with travel and high-roller hotel rooms.

For example, a video poker playing professional named David Walton recalled seeing Stephen Paddock at the Mandalay Bay Hotel and Casino in 2007. He remembered Paddock was interested in playing one specific machine – a Jacks-or-better 9-6 machine that paid 9-1 credits on a full house and 6-1 credits on a flush. That day, the casino was having a contest for a $100,000 drawing and players, based on the amount of their play the very next day, would get tickets to enter the contest. Walton saw some mistakes in Paddock's playing skills. For example, Paddock gave Walton inadequate advice on a hand when the two men were gambling at the Wynn Casino. But, when it came to persistence for winning the 24-hour contest at Mandalay Bay, Paddock would not be beat.

When Walton headed towards the Jacks-or-better machine, he recalled seeing Paddock sitting there. He wasn't playing it; he was just sitting there waiting to play it the minute the clock struck midnight and the contest officially began, Paddock started playing the machine at a rate of $120,000 per hour. Paddock played 24 hours straight and this obsessive playing paid off. When Walton checked the tickets for the contest, he only saw the same name over and over – Stephen Paddock. Paddock would end up winning the $100,000 contest at the Mandalay Bay that day way back in 2007, 10 years before he would return to that same hotel to murder innocent victims.

This was not the only fortunate time Stephen walked away with prizes through video game poker. Paddock was a regular at the Eureka Casino Resort in Mesquite and had won a $20,000 jackpot that was celebrated at the casino. He also once won a luxury car giveaway, although he ended up opting for a $90,000 cash prize in lieu of the vehicle. Paddock won another promotion several months later, this time leaving with a cash prize of $150,000.

Stephen Paddock was also known to have played at Caesars for years and earned the elite seven-star loyalty status through his constant gambling. This elite membership is reserved for only a select few players and comes with numerous benefits that Paddock was known to enjoy. From special gaming offers to free hotel stays and invites to exclusive events, the loyalty status Paddock attained is known as the ultimate accomplishment among Caesars gamblers. However, in 2006, the hotel and casino cut back on Paddock's elite offers and removed his favorite video game poker machines – the Ten Play Dollar and the Double Bonus Poker – because Paddock had become so skilled at knowing how to maximize his profits on those specific gambling machines. He was also known by a Caesars casino host to have a temper and had allegedly screamed at him spontaneously for his luggage being 20 minutes late to his presidential suite at the Rio. This was the room Paddock had occasionally requested and was a luxurious room with its own pool. The casino host had gotten to know Paddock, per his job to get to know the players, but said the conversations usually just stuck to gambling and traveling.

Stephen Paddock was not known as a "whale," a term used for only the highest rollers who tend to drop millions of dollars in a weekend, but he was known as a hefty better. Paddock would place bets that were impressive enough to take notice in Las Vegas's gambling world. On the Thursday night before the 2017 Las Vegas massacre, for example, he was seen in the high-limit room at Mandalay Bay playing machines that allowed players to bet $100 per hand of virtual poker cards. By his own admission, he would bet anywhere from $100 to $1,350 each time he pushed a video poker gambling machine button. He even praised a player nearby when the customer hit a royal flush before going back to his own hands.

Paddock had a methodical style of gambling that would, at times, help him win tens of thousands of dollars, attain hotel perks, and stay free-of-charge at some of the swankiest hotels and casinos in Las Vegas. According to his brother, Eric, Stephen was a math guy who viewed gambling as work – he knew how to calculate the odds and studied the math of gambling like it was his own form of education. This mathematical education and methodical way of living would pay off big when Stephen Paddock was gambling in Las Vegas. Stephen Paddock did not leave anything to chance; in fact, he even carried two cell phones – each with two different cell phone carriers – just in case one network would go down. He lived his life as he gambled, methodically and carefully.

Paddock was known to gamble in Strip hotels and even sued the upscale Cosmopolitan Las Vegas Luxury Hotel in 2011 for negligence, claiming that he sustained significant injuries in a fall on the hotel's property. Paddock claimed he fell due to an obstruction on the floor and hurt his hamstring, which then resulted in a lingering injury. He originally sued the hotel for $100,000 and had planned to cover more than $30,000 in medical bills from what he said was a hamstring tear and sprained wrist. He then sought damages of more than $10,000, but the arbitrator ruled against Paddock and the suit was dismissed in 2014 "with prejudice," which mean he could not bring the case up again. Despite that ruling, Stephen still spent quite a bit of time gambling and even claimed that his actual home was one of the casinos in which he stayed for free much of the time.

The 2013 deposition painted a grim picture of Paddock, but were they signs of the massacre he would inflict five years later? He gambled all night and slept all day and took Valium for his anxiousness (his Nevada doctor, Steven P. Winkler, was kept on retainer). He wagered up to $1 million a night gambling. He wore comfortable clothes like sweatpants and flip flops or khaki cotton pants and a polo shirt to further manage his anxiety and distress. If Paddock was seen in a button-down shirt and pants, he looked like he had been in the clothes for more than a few days. Paddock also never drove anything fancier than a standard rental car, and in the casinos he would even carry his own drinks to the high rollers area of the casinos and back to his room, or simply bring his own booze, so he would not need to over-tip the waitresses.

Federal government transactions also proved that Paddock was a high spender; there were dozens of currency transaction reports filed under his name, which means he had gambling transactions that were greater than $10,000. Paddock also had six-figure credit lines at casinos and was known as a reliable gambler who always paid his accounts. His big spending also procured rewards like comped rooms at luxury hotels, including his room at the Mandalay Bay Hotel and Casino in which he carried out his massacre. In fact, Paddock was known to hustle comps from hotels and really be in the gambling scene for the perks he received more than the money he was winnings. These kickbacks helped offset any losses Paddock may have endured during his gambling extravaganzas. For example, although the top machines at the Mandalay Bay Hotel and Casino pay out more than 99% for every $100 gambled, any losses can be offset by free food, free rooms, and other comped amenities. In the end, it would be a win-win for a professional gambler like Paddock, which was why he would consistently drive nearly 90 miles from his Mesquite home to the bright lights of Las Vegas.

Paddock made numerous large transactions leading up to his deadly shooting in 2017. He made gambling transactions in the sum of more than $10,000 a day (the amount that is required to be reported to the government) at multiple Las Vegas casinos and sometimes cleared more than $30,000 in one day. Although he was an avid gambler, those who knew him said he was a successful real estate investor and did not show any signs of having financial problems. But investigators later would find that finances may have been a motivator for mentally breaking in 2017.

GAMBLING TAKES A FINANCIAL TURN, NOT IN PADDOCK'S FAVOR

As time went on, winning at video poker became more and more difficult for Stephen Paddock, especially in Las Vegas. Machines with a better house advantage kept being added to casinos, making it harder to calculate winnings. The odds began to change at the machines, and they did not change in Stephen Paddock's favor. Investigators discovered that Paddock had made a reported $5 million in 2015, mostly from gambling. However, it was also found that between September 2015 and September 2017, Paddock's bank accounts had dropped by around $1.5 million.

Were financial issues a reason for the shooting? This was the one aspect of Paddock's personal profile that investigators would look at when trying to figure out his motive for committing such a horrific crime. Saying that Stephen Paddock had an unusual financial life was a bit of an understatement. Yes, he had two planes, owned multiple homes, and dropped tens of thousands of dollars at Las Vegas casinos on a consistent basis. He also gambled a total of at least $160,000 at Las Vegas casinos in the weeks leading up to his mass shooting. Did he have significant financial losses lead to Paddock's violence? More than likely, no.

Although Stephen Paddock did make several large gambling transactions in the weeks leading up to the massacre, there does not seem to be a connection. Yes, Paddock had recently gambled more than $10,000, $20,000, and even $30,000 a day at Las Vegas casinos. However, it was not clear what the wins and losses were or if there was any connection to his later actions. The only proof of winnings was a recent text message Stephen's brother, Eric, received from him that showed his brother had won $40,000. By all accounts, Stephen Paddock just seemed like an avid gambler with money to spare. As explained by Eric Madfis, an expert on mass murders in the United States who studies at the University of Washington in Tacoma, "mass killers do not just 'snap.'" However, Stephen Paddock did use his winnings for some very expensive purchases of a large gun collection.

LEADING UP TO THE MASS SHOOTING - WERE THERE SIGNS?

fter he committed the Las Vegas mass shooting, at least 19 additional firearms, explosives, and several thousand rounds of ammunition were found in Stephen Paddock's Mesquite home, while two shotguns and five handguns were found at his home in Reno. In total, police recovered 47 firearms from Paddock's hotel and his two homes. He legally purchased 33 of the 47 guns in four states, mostly rifles, in the 12 months leading up to the mass shooting, easily spending hundreds of thousands of dollars on guns. In fact, Paddock purchased all of his firearms that he used for his mass killing legally from the gun shops Dixie GunWorx and Guns & Guitars.

Chris Michel, the owner of Dixie GunWorx in St. George, Utah, said Paddock was similar to every other man who came in to buy guns. Michel explained that Paddock did not have any criminal record and had a reason for visiting his shop that he vocalized to others: "He was visiting all the local firearm shops is what he told everybody." Michel also said Paddock knew exactly what he was looking for when he came in, yet did not set off any alarms that he would use the weapons in a mass shooting. Paddock would visit the Dixie GunWorx a few times and, according to Michel, "He didn't set off any of my alarms, anything that I felt like there's a problem in any way, shape or form with him."

In addition, a representative from the Mesquite store, Guns & Guitars, said "he never gave any indication or reason to believe he was unstable or unfit at any time." It was clear that Stephen Paddock did not set off any alarms to anyone around him when he was stockpiling his arsenal. Paddock purchased three guns from Guns & Guitars, a handgun and two rifles, within a year. All of the purchases were legal and cleared routine federal screening. That is, all of the necessary background checks and procedures were followed, according to owner Chris Sullivan, and Paddock did not give him any indication that he was unstable or unfit to purchase the firearms. Guns & Guitars sells semi-automatic weapons, but not fully automatic weapons.

Both Sullivan and Michel would work with law enforcement and fully cooperate with federal authorities after the Las Vegas massacre. Yet, as Sullivan explained: "As for what goes on in a person's mind, I couldn't tell you...I know nothing about him personally." Stephen Paddock bought all of his guns legally and passed all background checks without signally any red flags. It seemed that even Paddock's closest confidants did not know him personally or the havoc and murder he would invoke on so many after purchasing his weapons.

In hindsight, Stephen Paddock did make some unusual requests at other gun stores. When Paddock and his girlfriend visited another gun shop, B&S Guns in Garland, Texas, he asked the salesman whether there was any way he could modify a gun so that it was easier to pull the trigger. This question also did not set off any red flags for owner, Paul Peddle, who recalled that Paddock had purchased handguns from his establishment before. On this day, Paddock's girlfriend, Dandy, was walking with a cane due to surgery and playing with Peddle's puppies while Paddock asked his questions.

Paddock had also approached an ammunition dealer at a gun show in Phoenix requesting a large quantity of tracer rounds, which are bullets that have a pyrotechnic charge that, when fired, leave an illuminated trace of its path. However, the dealer did not have the massive quantity he was requesting so Paddock did not buy anything from him. This was probably a blessing in disguise; if Paddock had used tracer bullets in his Las Vegas massacre, he would have been that much more precise of where his shots were going in the dark and could have been much more accurate and deadly. In fact, shooters who want better accuracy frequently mix tracer rounds with non-tracer rounds so that they have a weapon that can shoot accurately at a specific area. However, tracer rounds could have also helped police realize Paddock's location in the hotel since they would have been able to see more clearly where he was firing from in the dark. That being said, Paddock did not set off any red flags at the gun show – the dealer figured he just wanted the ammunition for recreational use – and Paddock would end up purchasing other ammunition at that show and then many guns, ammunition, and chemicals for bomb use from other various establishments.

Not only did gun shop owners not see any signs of distress, those working in the casinos Paddock frequented also did not notice any red flags. The weekend that Stephen Paddock committed his horrific mass shooting, an employee at the Mandalay Bay Resort and Casino said she served him for 16 hours during her shifts over the weekend. She said she had watched him gamble from Saturday to Sunday (the mass shooting took place Sunday night) and at one point she said he literally gambled for eight hours straight on high-stakes video poker machines in a separate, exclusive section of the casino. But this was not a surprise; this was simply the gambling life of Stephen Paddock. Yet, when she saw Paddock's face on the news identifying him as the suspected gunman who shot into a crowd of 22,000, she knew it was her customer the night before the deadly shooting.

Las Vegas prostitutes also provided a very telling description of Paddock, who they claimed was a regular customer. Similar to his treatment of the Las Vegas waitresses, the prostitutes also called Paddock a cheap man and said he did not display emotion during their encounters. One of these prostitutes was seen with Paddock in the days leading up to the Las Vegas massacre. Originally, investigators said Paddock was seen with another woman who was not his woman in the days leading up to the mass shooting. This woman ended up being identified as a prostitute, and she was not thought to have been in the hotel room with Paddock the night of the shooting.

Valium, also known as diazepam, has been on the market since 1963 and is known to have adverse effects. From rage and aggressiveness, to irritability and drowsiness, diazepam has been used to treat anxiety, seizures, muscle spasms, and the symptoms of alcohol withdraw. This type of anti-anxiety drug has also been used by marksmen to help calm their nerves while also steadying their aim. The link to diazepam and aggressionwas studied in a 1985 study of healthy male college students who saw their aggression intensified after taking the drug. These effects can be magnified by alcohol, and Paddock filled the prescription for this drug in 2016 and again in June of 2017, although that does not mean he was taking it on the night of the Las Vegas shooting. In addition, a pill bottle with a prescription for Valium was found during the shooting investigation.

Research has indicated that pathological gamblers such as Paddock can be diagnosed with psychopathic personality disorders and may have problems with alcohol. Yet, during the deposition,

Paddock claimed he rarely drank alcohol because, in his words, "at the stakes I play, you want to have all your wits about you, or as much wit as I have." During the months leading up to the shooting, people said they smelled alcohol on his breath from early in the morning and Stephen appeared to be despondent. When Paddock visited a car dealership in Reno, Nevada, he had allegedly told the salesman that he was depressed and was having troubles in his relationship. In addition, when he got his haircut at Great Clips a few months before the shooting, the hair dresser had described Paddock as smelling of alcohol while he explained how his girlfriend, who was also there, would be leaving to go to the Philippines. This was not uncommon, as the hairdresser described Paddock as smelling of alcohol each time she cut his hair. She attributed it to the all-night gambling he undertook so often, which he had even admitted to her on occasion. Other gamblers, and neighbors living in his Mesquite, Nevada, retirement community, also noted that Paddock was a drinker. Yet, the hairdresser also noticed that the relationship between Paddock and Hadley seemed cold and distant without any intimate interaction.

After the massacre, when Paddock's remains were sent to Stanford University, pathologists did not find any abnormalities present within the gunman's brain. Paddock's brain was damaged by the gunshot wound and there was some evidence of normal age-related changes, such as atherosclerosis, which reduces blood flow due to a narrowing of the arteries and fatty plaques inside the blood vessels. The only age-related finding that was interesting to the pathologists was called corpora amylacea, which is found in people who may be suffering from disorders like Alzheimer's, epilepsy, multiple sclerosis or a stroke. Again, this can be common in people in their 60s, but it was telling that his were in the frontal lobes and in such a high number. Yet, even those minor changes in Paddock's brain would not have explained any brain-related aggression, decision-making and impulse problems, or violent outbursts.

This would have more than likely been a blow to his brother, Eric, who had hoped they would find brain disease or something in his brain like a tumor that would have made the terror Stephen inflicted on so many even possible. But Stephen did not have any visual abnormalities in his brain. A diseased or damaged brain has been known to cause violent outbursts and acts since it can alter an individual's ability to control and regulate decision-making, impulses, and aggression. This is what was found in the brain of Charles Whitman, the former Marine who had killed 16 people on August 1, 1966 at the University of Texas at Austin after stabbing his wife and mother to death the night before. An autopsy of Whitman's brain revealed he had a tumor pressing against the part of the brain called the amygdala, which experts suggested caused the violent impulses he had been suffering from for years. However, this type of tumor was not found during the autopsy of Stephen Paddock, nor did Paddock have a stroke or any other neurological disorders that could have been a motive for his deadly actions. There could have been a number of neurological disorders that would encourage someone to violence, but none of them were found. In addition, experts would say that Stephen Paddock was not schizophrenic, which is usually a younger person's disorder that arises in the late teens or early twenties, not in someone's 60s. And, testimonials from family and friends of the killer do not paint a picture of a psychopath – someone who would send cookies and a walker to his mother, for example, is not usually the sign of a psychopathic killer.

43

A toxicology report did reveal that Stephen Paddock had anti-anxiety medication in his system based on a urine sample, but since it was not also detected in his blood it was not active. The only signs in the year leading up to the massacre could have been Stephen Paddock's gun purchases; according to the Bureau of Alcohol, Tobacco, Firearms and Explosives he purchased more than 55 firearms and a number of firearm-related accessories between October 2016 and September 28, 2017. This was a significant increase in Paddock's gun purchasing habits since he only purchased around 29 firearms, mainly handguns and shotguns, between 1982 and September 2016. Even though investigators would tell the media after the shooting that Paddock had been stockpiling weapons since 1982, the majority of them, mostly rifles, were purchased during the year leading up to the deadly massacre on October 1, 2017.

His girlfriend, Dandy, did notice the increase in firearm-related purchased, but thought it was just an increase in his hobby. So, at Paddock's request, she traveled to her native country, the Philippines, after he bought her a surprise airline ticket. Dandy also did not see any red flags when he wired her $100,000 to buy a house there; instead, she thought it was a sign he was ending his relationship with her. According to Dandy, "It never occurred to me in any way whatsoever that he was planning violence against anyone." With Dandy out of the way, a home surveillance system showed Paddock driving alone to an area near his home for target practice two days before the shooting.

Although Dandy claimed she had no hint or clue that her boyfriend was about to commit the most horrific mass shooting in America's history, others who knew him did see a slight deterioration in his demeanor in the months leading up to the shooting. Among other things, investigators were told that Paddock's mental state had been deteriorating in the months leading up to the mass shooting, he had begun gaining weight and having an increasingly sloppy and disheveled appearance, and he even started becoming obsessed with Danley's ex-husband. Someone even was quoted as stating that Paddock was "descending into madness," a powerful description of what could have been a motive – Paddock's deteriorating mental state.

A British tourist visiting Las Vegas claimed to have an encounter with Paddock the night before the shooting. He said Paddock was strange – making references to biblical scripture, saying God would come down and save men who were down on their luck, and even said he once tried to commit suicide by burning himself to death. The tourist also remembered the individual, who he believed to be Paddock, actually admitting he wanted to die and complaining that he had a younger girlfriend who always wanted to have sex (although Danley would tell authorities that their relationship was no longer intimate). Some of Paddock's friends and family said he told them he was feeling fatigued and ill, and even his girlfriend mentioned he was acting strange in the weeks leading up to the mass shooting.

Another man said he was confronted by Paddock around 10:00 p.m. at a bus stop right before the shooting. He claimed Paddock asked him if he believed in God before telling him to say a prayer for what was about to happen that night and asked how he could get a ticket into the country music festival. In addition, three days before the shooting a woman claimed to have heard Paddock talking to a man at a Las Vegas restaurant about standoffs: the 1992 Ruby Ridge standoff in Idaho in which a right-wing activist had an 11 day standoff with authorities, and the 51 day standoff at Waco, Texas, between a Christian cult and police in 1993. The later standoff resulted in 80 deaths, including 22 children. She said Paddock appeared angry and made her want to leave the restaurant.

A sheriff investigating the case also questioned whether a mental condition ran in Paddock's family, calling his younger brother, Eric, "manic" and inquiring whether something was associated with the family itself. Stephen's other brother, Bruce, was arrested a few weeks after the shooting on suspicion of possessing child pornography. His third brother, Patrick, however, had not been in contact with Stephen for 20 years and he did not even recognize his brother initially when he saw his picture on television as the mass shooter. Others who knew Stephen Paddock simply connected this deterioration to losing a significant amount of money in the years leading up to the Las Vegas shooting. If this was the case, however, how did the person closest to Paddock – his own girlfriend – not notice this deterioration?

THAT FATEFUL NIGHT –
OCTOBER 1, 2017

I
t is not surprising why Stephen Paddock ultimately chose the Las Vegas Strip and the Route 91 Harvest Festival as the target for his mass shooting. Paddock had researched numerous festivals and areas that had large amounts of people at once. The Las Vegas Strip is a very popular stretch of the famous Las Vegas Boulevard immediately south of the city of Las Vegas. It is well-known as a highly concentrated area of resort hotels and casinos – highly concentrated in both the buildings and large amounts of tourists who visit every year with the hopes of winning big. One of those popular resorts and casinos is the 43-story Mandalay Bay, which is located southwest of its intersection with Mandalay Bay Road in Paradise, and independent, unincorporated town. Then there is what is known as Las Vegas Village, which is a 15-acre venue used for outdoor performances. Paddock's girlfriend had remembered that he had repeatedly cased out this area of Las Vegas Village from different windows in their room when they had stayed at the Mandalay Bay Hotel and Casino about a month before his vicious attack. Yet, nothing about those movements seemed out of the ordinary at the time.

This country music festival has been held at the Las Vegas Village and Festival Grounds since 2014, operated by MGM Resorts, and covered the impressive 15 acres and had a 40,000-person capacity. The festival's website had promoted that the three-day concert was sold out, and the shooting fell on the final day of the event. The gunman was only a few hundred yards northeast of the festival in the Mandalay Bay Las Vegas Hotel and Casino. The luxury resort opened in 1999 and, since that time, has become one of Las Vegas's most prestigious hotels and casinos. No one could have imagined the lavish property would also become the home to the deadliest mass shooting by a sole gunman in United States history.

At 10:05 p.m. on a warm Sunday night, October 1, 2017, Paddock acted alone and opened fire on people attending the three-day country music event, the Route 91 Harvest Music Festival. This was seen on CCTV from the concert venue. A guest on the 30th floor, two floors down from the shooting, thought he heard fireworks going off before texting a friend and calling his father asking him to contact the Las Vegas police. Even on the 30th floor, the walls and windows were vibrating from the deadly shooting two floors above. Even individuals who were inside the Luxor Hotel-Casino, which was directly north of the festival, were found running and crying due to the gun shots outside.

Some concertgoers thought the noise was made from fireworks; for example, one woman, a 41-year-old from California, said she was drinking and laughing with friends at the concert when they heard what they thought was fireworks. It was not until she saw a man near them who fell to the ground, blood coming from his neck. According to this witness, "It seemed like rapid fire...There was blood pouring everywhere." Another concertgoer from Boise, Idaho, also said that numerous people around her thought they were hearing fireworks, but she knew immediately that those sounds were not fireworks. Her mother threw her to the ground, and they were worried they could be trampled as people started running out of the festival venue. The mom and daughter followed suit and rushed to leave the danger they knew was surrounding them.

Another woman also said she thought she was hearing firecrackers, but when the "pop pop pop" kept going, her husband told her those noises were not firecrackers. He told her it sounded like someone was shooting from a semi-automatic rifle. There were other attendees who were skeptical of the fireworks theory. One concertgoer had said she knew immediately that the bangs were not made by fireworks before her mother threw her on the ground and laid on top of her to protect her. She knew something was terribly wrong.

Still, another man who was near the stage when the shooting started also initially thought the sounds were simply fireworks. He only realized that something was wrong when the stage went dark. Then, when event staff pulled headliner Jason Aldean off the stage, he dropped and ran for safety. He only then realized the sounds were gunshots and that he had to escape for his life. He ran towards the perimeter of the fence where someone in a truck used their vehicle to rip down the fence so that crowd members had a chance of survival. Still others who were simply dancing and having a great time also thought the sounds were coming from a fireworks show. It was only when people started falling and there was blood everywhere that the realization came – these were gun shots, not fireworks.

Confusion immediately arose as online video captured the country music stopping and attendees yelling at people to get down and stay down – some concertgoers thought it was simply fireworks and rejected the evacuation requests from law enforcement. Others yelled expletives and began running in fear. Officers plead with civilians to run for cover as the gunfire erupted and victims began to fall, bleeding and fighting for their lives. As gunfire cracked for nearly 11 minutes, officers would strain to find the source of the shots. A family friendly country music concert turned into sheer chaos, people yelling, running, screaming, and dying. Concertgoers would run for their lives, jumping fences to scramble to safety into the city streets, as bullets sprayed the area below. Video even showed nine seconds of continuous rapid fire, 37 seconds of silence while screaming could be heard, and then gunfire erupting again and again. In the end, a gunman would fire more than 1,000 rounds from a hotel room above the crowd.

Within two-and-a-half minutes, firefighters rushed to figure out where the gunfire was coming from and a mass-casualty incident unit was requested to the concert. However, it would take a total of 75 minutes (it was originally reported as 72 minutes) from the moment the shooting started for officers to affirm that the shooting was over. When the first call about the shooting came in across the Las Vegas radio channel, it stated in a rush of static that shots were fired and they sounded like they were coming from an automatic firearm. Police were fielding reports of multiple shooters and mass casualties within minutes after Paddock began firing. Because the reports were stating that there was more than one shooter, officers believed there were suspects on more than one floor of the Mandalay Bay. The police cleared out the Mandalay Bay's 29th floor before working their way up to the 32nd floor where Stephen Paddock was staying. But, questions would end up arising as to why officers had locked down the 32nd floor and were at Paddock's hotel door at 10:25 p.m. but waited until nearly an hour later, around 11:21 p.m., to forcefully enter the killer's hotel room.

The officers would go on the CBS show "60 Minutes" to discuss what they encountered on that night. These officers were the first ones to see Paddock's dead body, surrounded by a murderous arsenal. The officers told the CBS correspondent that it was "very eerie" walking into Paddock's hotel room and how it looked straight "out of a movie."

THE TIMELINE OF TRAGEDY

The first reports of the mass shooting came across police radio channels at 10:08 p.m. local Pacific time. Officers could be heard over police radio saying that they were being pinned down by gunfire. Just before midnight, Las Vegas police reported that they had a suspect down and they did not believe there were any other active gunmen. The question remains, however, as to what took so long between when shots were reported and nearly two hours later when Stephen Paddock's body was found and the area was finally secured.

At 10:12 p.m., the first two officers arrived on the 31st floor of the Mandalay Bay Hotel and Casino and announced that the gunfire was coming from the floor above them. At 10:15 p.m. the last shots were fired by Paddock and two minutes later, at 10:17 p.m., the first two officers arrived on the 32nd floor. At 10:18 p.m., security officer Jesus Campos told the officers he was shot and told them exactly what room the gunman is staying in on the 32nd floor. Campos had responded to an open-door alert on the 32nd floor at the beginning of the shooting. Once he had arrived on the floor using the stairwell, he realized he could not get past a barricade blocking the entrance. So, Campos used the elevator and then entered the 32nd floor to a barrage of gunfire. While walking through the hall, Paddock must have seen him on his cameras and shot Campos through the hotel door, hitting him in the leg.

Eight additional officers would arrive on the 32nd floor around 10:25 p.m. and, using a master key card, started systematically clearing every room while looking for anyone who may have been injured. However, officers would not enter the hotel room of Stephen Paddock until 11:20 p.m., more than an hour after he fired his first shot into the crowd of 22,000 people. The officers would find Paddock lying on the floor, dead, from a self-inflicted gunshot wound to the head. Now, police actions are usually critiqued after something tragic like a mass shooting. For example, the police's actions and delayed responses during both the Columbine attacks and the Pulse nightclub mass shooting in Orlando were both met with criticisms. Some criticisms would also arise after Stephen Paddock was found to be already killed by a self-inflicted gunshot wound to the head.

A CALCULATED PLAN

L eading up to October 1st, Paddock would have overlapping reservations at a downtown Las Vegas high-rise condo and the Mandalay Bay, spending time at both locations. He also traveled back to his homes in Reno, Mesquite, and in Arizona. Police would originally report that Paddock had been staying in the hotel since September 28th, but would later revise the date to Monday, September 25th, a week before his deadly shooting. Paddock checked into the Mandalay Bay Las Vegas Hotel and Casino on September 25th, six days prior to the shooting. His stay, which would have normally cost $590 per night, was comped by the hotel, and he had requested a room on a higher floor overlooking the country music festival. This gave him a vantage point that increased the likelihood that even inaccurate gunshots would still hit someone. Paddock then moved into an additional suite, room 32-135, connected to his first one, room 32-134, on Thursday, September 29th, three nights before the fateful massacre. Both rooms overlooked the country music festival grounds, allowing him to point his weapons over objects and obstacles that people could have normally used to hide for cover.

Paddock had even made two noise complaints the night before the shooting about the guest below him in room 31-135, Albert Garzon, who was playing country music. Garzon, a restaurant owner from San Diego, said he did turn down the music after security guards knocked on his door at 1:30 a.m. Sunday. Then, around 2 a.m., another set of guards showed up at his hotel door and he turned his music off. Although the guards had told Garzon that the guest above him had complained, he had no idea it was the perpetrator of the deadliest mass shooting in United States history until early Monday morning. According to Garzon, "I looked up and I could see his curtain flapping in the wind."

Although room service was served during his stay – he would pretend like he was talking to other people in his room when he was ordering and checking their orders – Paddock kept the "Do Not Disturb" sign on the door over those three days and nights so that no one would enter the room – no cleaning, no room service, nothing. In fact, housekeepers are only allowed to enter a room with the "Do Not Disturb" sign if they are accompanied by a security guard and only after several days of no cleaning, so this alone was not suspicious to those working in the hotel nor did it raise a red flag for workers. There was only one housekeeper who had described how uncomfortable Paddock had made her when she was cleaning out the refrigerator and changing the bed sheets, at his request. Paddock had ordered room service, and after he received his mean she said he kept staring at her while she was cleaning his room four days before the mass shooting. She said she also found it unusual that one man had five pieces of luggage in his room. In the end, however, even though Paddock had, at a minimum, 10 suitcases in his room that contained a large supply of weaponry and equipment for his massacre – from firearms and ammunition to computers and video cameras – he could have easily brought them in at different times over the next few days without provoking suspicion.

Stephen Paddock wore black pants and a black glove on the night of October 1, 2017. He positioned himself in front of his hotel room's floor-to-ceiling windows that showed a perfect view of the country music crowd listening to singer Jason Aldean. Men and women were swaying to the music, kids were sitting on their parents' shoulders – no one saw it coming. He made sure to have a circle of surveillance around him, with cameras outside of his room, including one on a service cart, and one at his hotel door's peephole to look for anyone who may approach him from behind. At one point, he used tools and metal bars that he brought with him to the hotel to barricade the doors to his room and the stairwell of the 32nd floor.

At one point, the baby monitor camera that was placed on the service cart outside of his room must have shown the hotel's unarmed security guard Jesus Campos. Campos was called to the floor because a door-ajar alarm was going off, so the unarmed security guard attempted to enter the 32nd floor at 9:59 p.m., minutes before the massacre began. Campos instead encountered around 35 rounds of gunfire through Paddock's door. Campos had attempted to enter the floor on an unrelated matter and found that Paddock had screwed the door to the hallway shut. Campos was wounded, stating that he was hit by something in his left back calf; it was later noted that Paddock shot through the door and hit Campos in the leg while he was checking on an alarm a few doors down from Paddock's room. Yet, Campos was still able to radio police for help, even with his injury, and was called a hero by law enforcement representatives. The alarm that Campos went to check was more than likely a fortunate coincidence; that room a few doors down did not have a door forced open – it seemed to be open for a while – and Paddock did not have keys to that room. But the shooting seemed to stop when Paddock saw Campos. Up until then, Paddock was free to complete his horrific mass shooting by having all eyes on the hallways and the grounds below. In all accounts, Paddock had a well-planned massacre; he brought 10 pieces of luggage filled with weapons and specifically requested an upper-floor room overlooking the venue. And this was only after researching numerous, largely populated targets.

At 10:05 p.m., gunfire from what sounded like an automatic weapon rained down on concertgoers of the Route 91 Harvest music festival. This was exactly when Stephen Paddock started firing hundreds of rounds, in rapid succession using his modified rifles, into the crowd of 22,000 below. When the shooting started, no one saw it coming. Paddock appeared to have used a hammer-like weapon to smash his hotel windows so that he could get a more clear shot on the festival's crowd. A Metro detective looked up at the Mandalay Bay Las Vegas Hotel and Casino with a pair of binoculars and saw what he described as "a silhouette of a male standing in a shooting position several feet back from a window." Paddock opened fire on the crowd about an hour after a version of "God Bless America" had played, and his slaughter lasted for between nine and 11 minutes. It has been speculated that the massive killing spree stopped because Paddock took his own life, shooting himself through the mouth. When the police found Paddock, he was lying dead, blood from a head wound, among dozens of cartridge casings and a revolver lying near him.

The first two police officers to reach the 32nd floor of the Mandalay Bay Las Vegas Hotel and Casino at 10:17 p.m. – more than 10 minutes after Stephen Paddock started his massacre. At 10:18 p.m. the officers arrived at Paddock's hotel door, and between 10:26 and 10:30 p.m. eight more Las Vegas officers arrived and began clearing the 32nd floor hallway. It was not until nearly 11:00 p.m. that eight SWAT team members would also enter the 32nd floor of the hotel and casino through the stairwell that was closest to Paddock's suite. Together, the officers cleared all of the other rooms on the 32nd floor. At 11:20 p.m. – more than an hour after Stephen Paddock began his murderous rampage – the SWAT team used explosives to penetrate the hotel door of Paddock and found the gunman dead inside his suite. Paddock died by suicide from a self-inflicted gunshot wound to the head.

In all accounts, it did not seem that this was a suicide mission; although Paddock did leave a note on the nightstand near one of the windows that he smashed with a hammer in order to fire into the crowd. However, it was confirmed it was not a suicide note nor did it give any inclining to his motivations for the killings. Instead, investigators found a note in Paddock's room that had handwritten calculations of where he needed to aim for maximized accuracy to kill as many people as possible. Also on the note were calculations of the target distance, his elevation in the room, and even the bullet trajectory compared to the line of fire. In fact, the calculations detailed the drop of what his bullet would be, further detailing where to shoot his targets. So, Paddock did not plan on dying that day, as illustrated in his note, but instead was trying to calculate how to kill as many innocent victims as possible by computing how to attack the specific crowd size based on trajectory and distance.

Authorities would also conclude that Stephen Paddock did not have any connections with a terrorist group, such as the ISIS claim, and that he had planned his attack without any terrorist group motivations or accomplices. At first, the Islamic State of Iraq and the Levant (ISIL), also known as the Islamic State of Iraq and Syria (ISIS), claimed responsibility for the attack and connected Paddock to their organization. The Islamic State had asserted that Paddock converted to Islam six months before the attack and was identified now as Abu Abdul Barr al-Amriki. In fact, U.S. Representative Scott Perry, a Republican from Pennsylvania, also claimed in a national television appearance to have evidence that suggested the Islamic State was connected to the Las Vegas shooting. However, the Federal Bureau of Investigation would not find any connection between Paddock and the international terrorist group after seizing his computer hard drives and examining dozens of weapons from the hotel suite.

Although the FBI would later debunk these claims, the Islamic State militant group would even publish an infographic called "The Invasion of Las Vegas" in its weekly "Al-Naba" online magazine which detailed how the jihadists arranged and coordinated the Las Vegas shooting. The information was intended to further strengthen the claims that Stephen Paddock had converted to Islam before killing 58 people in the worst mass shooting in United States history (although the terrorist group would use a wrong number that was misinformed by the media in the beginning of the investigation – 59 people).

The publication reiterated how Paddock was a soldier of the Islamic State caliphate called Abu Abdul Barr al-Amriki and had allegedly converted to Islam. A caliphate is a state that is governed in accordance with Islamic law, or Sharia. The caliphate has commanded Muslims all across the globe to swear their allegiance to the group's leader, Ibrahim Awad Ibrahim al-Badri al-Samarrai (also known as Abu Bakr al-Baghdadi) and travel to the area that is under its control. The Islamic State has sought to destroy obstacles to, what they claim, would restore God's rule on Earth and defend the Muslim community from infidels and apostates. Although the militant group claimed that Stephen Paddock was an Islamic State caliphate soldier, the group, however, did not offer any proof to back up their publication's claim. The only claim of any evidence to connect Paddock to the terrorist group said there was a "source," but kept it at just that, was from the terror group's Amaq news agency. That news outlet asserted that Paddock had responded to calls to target Coalition countries and then later also claimed he had converted to Islam months before the attack. On September 10, 2014, the United States had announced that it would form a broad international coalition to defeat ISIS. However, the group's media outlet did not specify who the source was that connected Paddock to this coalition. Instead, this phrase was in reference to a famous speech in 2014, in which former Islamic State spokesman Abu

Muhammad al-Adnani called out for sympathizers across the globe to carry out violence against countries that are fighting against ISIS.

Experts noted that this was not the first time the terrorist group would take responsibility to an unrelated attack against innocent American victims. The Islamic State has claimed that violence carried out by either those targeted by the terrorist group directly, or indirectly by those who were inspired by their ideology. However, recently the terrorist group has made a few false claims that have later been debunked. The terrorist group had also falsely claimed they were behind an attack on a casino in Manila, a botched robbery in the Philippines, and a bomb plot at the Charles de Gaulle Airport in Paris. This was a common strategy the extremists had embarked on and would prove to be a false claim as it related to the murderous actions of Stephen Paddock. The FBI would report that they did not find any proof that he had any links to any international terrorist organization, let alone the Islamic State.

In addition to firearms, officers also found pounds of ammonium nitrate fertilizer, which can be used to make improvised explosive devices and homemade bombs, pounds upon pounds of Tannerite, used to make explosive targets, and 1,600 rounds of ammunition in Stephen Paddock's car, a 2017 Chrysler Pacifica Touring, at the hotel after the shooting took place. Officers did note, however, that Paddock did not seem to have assembled any explosive devices. Yet, officers continued to try to find a motive, searching Paddock's second home in northern Nevada and questioned numerous relatives and associates, but found nothing. No reason for the killings.

From what law enforcement found, including gas masks in his room and 1,600 rounds of ammunition, chemicals, and 50 pounds of explosives in his car that was parked in the hotel parking lot, it appeared that Paddock had planned to survive his massive attack and escape unharmed. Although the explosives and chemicals found in his car could have been used to make a bomb, law enforcement officials said they did not know what he was planning with the 50 pounds of explosives found in his car, as it seemed he was just using the guns and ammunition for the mass shooting over the country music festival. In any case, he may have had the explosives when he escaped from this massacre so that he was equipped for additional assaults he could have been planning after the Las Vegas mass shooting. This supposition is because some experts have said there are only three conclusions to a mass shooting: suicide, a shoot-out with police, or an escape to continue preplanned killings. If Paddock had planned to escape, the third option, using the additional guns, ammunition, and explosions, made sense. However, he may not have planned as well as he thought; Paddock rented the hotel room in his own name and he was spotted on numerous cameras throughout the Mandalay Bay Hotel and Casino. If Paddock would have escaped his deadly massacre, he would have more than likely still have been a wanted man.

The FBI and the Department of Homeland Security would work with investigators to figure out why the Las Vegas shooting occurred. Investigators were also researching whether Stephen Paddock was planning another attack before he decided on the Las Vegas concert festival. There were a number of laptops in his suite, with one missing a hard drive. Paddock's online history, reviewed by Metro police, was disturbing, containing research on potential targets in Chicago, Boston, and Santa Monica, and possible venues in Las Vegas. He had also researched hotel rooms near Fenway Park in Boston (home of the Red Sox) and had allegedly reserved two rooms at the Blackstone Hotel on South Michigan Avenue in Chicago in August, across the street and the same weekend of the site of the Lollapalooza music festival. This music festival, held from August 3 through August 6, was set to attract hundreds of thousands of people, including one of former President Barack Obama's daughters. According to the hotel, Paddock never checked in that weekend and, instead, cancelled days before the concert. He did, however, scout another music festival in Las Vegas that was taking place the weekend before the country music festival.

Officials found that Paddock had rented a room at the Ogden (through Airbnb), a luxury condominium tower in downtown Las Vegas between September 17 and September 28 during the Life is Beautiful Festival held September 22 through 24 and headlined by the musical acts Lorde, the Gorillaz, and Chance the Rapper. The condos were on high floors and overlooked the music festival. In addition, security footage even showed him bringing multiple suitcases into the Ogden, possibly to transport weapons (just like he did during his stay at Mandalay Bay). He also tried to get a hotel room at the El Cortez, but it was booked, and he specifically researched the number of attendees at other concerts being held in Las Vegas as well as the size of crowds that attend Santa Monica's beach.

His search history also showed research on munitions and tactics, SWAT tactics, as well as hundreds of photographs of child pornography. A few weeks later, on October 25, 2017, Stephen Paddock's brother, Bruce, 58, was arrested in North Hollywood, California, on charges of possessing more than 600 explicit child pornography images in 2014 (at least 10 of them were of children younger than 12 years of age) and had also swapped pornography with others. The images predated his brother's shooting and were found inside a building that Bruce Paddock was squatting in, but at the time he could not be found. When he was found after his brother committed the horrific mass shooting, he was detained at a Los Angeles assisted-living facility where he was waiting to have surgery for spinal stenosis. Bruce Paddock faced 19 counts of sexual exploitation of a child and one count of child pornography and was even held on a $60,000 bond. Those charges were dropped in May 2018. Now that a magnifying glass was on Bruce, due to his brother's mass shooting, court records also revealed he had a criminal record that stretched back to the 1980s for criminal threats, vandalism, theft, and driving with a suspended vehicle, to name a few of the 20 criminal charges against him. Bruce was obviously not happy that his brother's dreadful crime had brought attention to Bruce's offenses. Bruce had been estranged from his family but did try to reconnect with both his brother Eric and Stephen's girlfriend, Marilou Danley, after the mass shooting in Las Vegas.

Country music star Jason Aldean was the headliner of the three-day country music event and was performing on stage at the time of the shooting – around 10 p.m. Aldean had been a country music sensation for more than 10 years since his debut single release in 2005, "Hicktown." On October 1, 2017, Aldean had just begun performing his hit "When She Says Baby" when Paddock began firing into the crowd of more than 22,000 concertgoers. Video showed the events unfold; shots were heard to be rapidly firing, pop-pop-pop-pop, Aldean stopped playing his song, and the crowd, at first, got quiet. Then, the madness started – Paddock fired a volley of bullets, victims fell to the ground, and others bolted in panic.

His music stopped, concertgoers screamed and ducked for cover, and victims began falling and bleeding as they were shot. Some victims hid behind concession stands while others crawled under parked cars for safety. Video would later show the 40-year-old singer running from the stage as the gunfire broke out into the audience. Jake Owen, a country singer who was on stage with Aldean, told the media that he was not exaggerating when he claimed the shooting went on for at least 10 minutes and that it was like "shooting fish in a barrel from where he was."

IT WAS "BEYOND HORRIFIC"

"**B**eyond horrific" were the words of Jason Aldean when he was describing what he saw that fateful night. Aldean would end up canceling the rest of his upcoming shows for the weekend. Concertgoers listening to Aldean would explain the "pop, pop, pop" they heard, stepping over the individuals lying on the ground, dead, people screaming, blood everywhere. The shooting seemed to come from an automatic rifle – volleys that lasted about 10 seconds over a period of about 10 minutes.

Police would shut down the popular Las Vegas Boulevard while authorities from across Nevada would join local Las Vegas officials rushing to the scene. The south end of the Las Vegas strip and freeway traffic on I-15 from the Tropicana to Russell Road would be shut down, and more than 25 flights intended for McCarran Airport, which is located on Wayne Newton Boulevard in Las Vegas, were diverted due to the reported shooting. Around 300 people fled into the airport to escape the shooting, prompting airport officials to shut down all four of the airport's runways. Early reports also stated that Paddock shot at fuel tanks at McCarran International Airport from his hotel window and, as such, the airport was reviewing safety measures. The airport did state that there was a low probability that the fuel tanks could be ignited by gun fire.

The casualties during the approximately 10 minutes of carnage would accumulate at an incredible rate, with bystanders, policemen, nurses, current and former military individuals, anyone who was willing, tending to the wounded. As one witness said, "Everyone was running, you could see people getting shot...I've never been that scared in my life." She was not exaggerating her fear, as people were shot in the legs, head, chest, blood was everywhere. Even hotel guests on the same floor could smell the gun powder and were taken aback by the gun shots that just kept going and going.

THE VICTIMS' STORIES

Stephen Paddock had a large amount of time to fire long, rapid-fire bursts from what seemed like using a machine-type gun. Concert attendees ran and screamed for their lives as bullets flew everywhere and the panicked concertgoers rushed to escape the carnage. One woman saw people running and screaming and, even though she was wearing a boot for a broken foot, ran with her parents towards a fence with a hole in it. While waiting to get through the hole to safety, she felt a burning in her hip – she had been shot. Another man, who was at the concert with his mother, knew the sounds he heard were gun shots right away and began running. Suddenly, he felt something hit his foot and later realized it was a piece of shrapnel that was lodged into his boot and injured his toe. Another man told police he had called his wife to tell her he did not know if he would be making it home because shots were coming from everywhere.

These are just a few of the stories of 22,000 concertgoers trying to flee the mass shooting.

Other concertgoers were not injured by gunshots, but instead by other scared people trying to run to safety. One local woman had been knocked down during the chaos and individuals kept stepping on her ankle. She was not sure if she would survive the trampling before she was finally able to get up and escape. Hysterical concertgoers were literally piling on top of each other trying to escape Stephen Paddock's constant gunshots.

Not all concertgoers were fleeing without helping others – many of them tried to help the injured, such as a female server who saw a woman bleeding and then took off her own tank top to use as a tourniquet. Another woman said two people gave a bandana and jean jacket to her so that she could stop the bleeding of her husband's wound. Finally, another concertgoer from San Diego saw people bleeding all around him and knew he had to do something to save lives. He ran into the parking lot adjacent from the concert fairgrounds, found a festival truck with keys in it, and used it to transport nearly 30 critically injured victims to the hospital. When a husband and wife made it to their car, they found people hiding underneath. The couple ended up putting as many people as they could in their car, some without shoes, so that they could all drive to safety. All around the chaos there were individuals holding people's wounds shut and shielding total strangers from the gunfire.

Blood was everywhere and the victims kept falling to the ground. One woman saw a girl standing right next to her fall down. The victim grabbed her stomach and her hands were all bloody. The poor girl screamed and then just fell back. Another concertgoer saw a man with a bullet wound in his neck, not moving at all. People just started dropping as the gunshots kept coming and coming. The firing seemed to go on forever, and all around on the ground were purses, shoes, and bodies covered in blood.

One woman threw herself on top of her brother and told her she loved him. Luckily, both would survive the mass shooting. Another man said he survived only by jumping into a walk-in freezer at the Mandalay Bay Hotel and Casino, which was already filled with around 30 concertgoers trying to hide from the mayhem. A festival worker who was working behind the stage when the shooting started hid with others in a trailer where she saw people already helping the injured by using their belts as tourniquets to stop the bleeding.

Another woman from Huntington Beach, California, was attending the concert with her daughter-in-law and three children, one with whom was disabled. The family was sitting in the area designated for the disabled when the gunfire started. She ran with her son carrying her daughter towards the perimeter fence and the family were able to push a section of the fence over with the help of others trying to flee the scene. She ran with her family into a hangar at the McCarran International Airport where about 100 concertgoers were already hiding for safety.

This fateful night was the result of one man: Stephen Paddock.

In the end, 58 individuals and the gunman would be dead, more than 800 would be injured, more than 400 being directly injured from gunfire, and the United States of America would face its largest and deadliest mass shooting to date.

Victims from California who attended the Route 91 Harvest Music Festival did get an opportunity to apply for monetary support for victims of violent crimes. The help was available for the survivors of those who were killed at the concert, anyone who was injured, and those in attendance, as well as their immediate family members. The money, which is up to $70,000 per victim, was allocated to help pay for any lost wages suffered, medical bills, mental health treatment, and funeral expenses. In addition, online fundraisers would collect millions of dollars for the Las Vegas shooting victims. After the tragedy, the website GoFundMe had dozens of campaigns for the victims, raising millions of dollars for them and their families.

Some families also sought solace from Paddock's own estate. For example, the family of Travis Phippen asked a Nevada court to appoint a special administrator to take control of Paddock's assets, in part, to make the monies available for any future lawsuits that may be filed by his shooting victims. Travis was attending the concert with his father, John, and when the shooting started Travis, who was a medic, stopped to help someone. John stayed with his son and was shielding the woman when his son was shot dead by Paddock. MGM Resorts International, which owns the Mandalay Bay Hotel and Casino, would also agree to pay up to $800 million to settle lawsuits from victims of the mass shooting.

THE AFTERMATH

By Monday morning, the Mandalay Bay Hotel and Casino was on partial lockdown. The exits to the Las Vegas Strip were closed, and guests could only enter the hotel through the parking area in the back. The casino floor would be largely empty, and several guests were seen sleeping on couches with only towels or bathrobes available to cover them. Everyone was reeling from the murderous events that had happened the night before. The valet had been shut down, and Stephen Paddock's own vehicle was still there.

As survivors began to filter out of the venue, they left a scene of horror. People were scrunched on the ground after being shot, victims trampling over others to run for their lives, some heroes even stopping to shield total strangers from gunfire while others provided aid to the wounded. First it was reported that at least 20 individuals had died. Then the number was updated to say "in excess of 50." For a while after that, the media reported that 58 people lost their lives on the fateful night of the Route 91 Harvest Festival concert (there was confusion in the media, however, with many reporting that the final number was 59). The final number then jumped by one more than two years later when a 57-year-old woman, Mira Loma of California, died at Redlands Community Hospital. Loma was paralyzed in the shooting, passing away on November 15, 2019.

In the end, Stephen Paddock killed 58 innocent victims – 36 women and 22 men – with ages ranging from the youngest victim, 20 years old, to the oldest victim who was killed at age 67, and fired a total of 1,057 shots. Thirty-one of the 58 victims killed were pronounced dead at the scene and the other 27 died at the hospital. In total, 35 of those killed were from California, six were from Nevada, four were from Canada, two were from Alaska, two were from Utah, and one concertgoer who lost his or her life were each from Arizona, Colorado, Iowa, Massachusetts, Minnesota, New Mexico, Pennsylvania, Tennessee, Washington, West Virginia, and Wisconsin. All of these victims died of gunshot wounds at the hands of Stephen Paddock.

A kindergarten teacher, a special education teacher, a nurse, a Las Vegas police officer, a secretary, a retiree; these were just a few of the nearly 60 people who lost their lives on that fateful day. Two off-duty police officers who were attending the concert were also killed and two on-duty officers were wounded. More than 800 people were injured, with more than 500 being directly injured from gun fire.

Nearly a week after the horror unfolded, the back half of the venue, which was the size of a football field, was littered with personal items, chairs, and other remains. Federal agents would begin carrying out and loading into trucks piles of purses, backpacks, strollers, and lawn chairs that were left behind at the concert venue. They would try to return as many personal items as possible to those who had survived the mass shooting, or to those who lost loved ones.

Patients surged into the area's hospitals – Sunrise Hospital and Medical Center, the University Medical Center of Southern Nevada, and at least one of the six hospitals of the Valley Health System. Most of the victims – 199 – were rushed to the Sunrise Hospital and Medical Center, the main hospital that was within walking distance from where the Route 91 Harvest Music

Festival was held. Within the first 40 minutes, 150 patients would arrive at the Level Two trauma center, a designation given to medical centers that are able to give care for all injured patients. Part of this rush was due to some miscommunication by the emergency services announcement, which erroneously broadcasted that the University Medical Center of Southern Nevada had reached capacity. This Level 1 trauma center was also hard to access for more than half of the victims needing care because they were traveling by car and Interstate 15, which was the most direct road from the festival's location, was closed to the public. Due to the confusion and road closures, most patients were rerouted to Sunrise Hospital and Medical Center and by noon the next day, the total of patients at the medical facility ballooned to 180 injured individuals. Patients were sorted based on a one (most critical) to five ratio to handle the influx of the wounded. Sadly, a separate area had to be created for concertgoers who doctors considered to be "unsalvageable." Of the 199 patients that would end up flooding the Sunrise Hospital and Medical Center, 124 had met the criteria for what was called trauma activation, which meant they included patients with either single or multiple gunshot wounds. They included patients with gunshot wounds to the face, head, chest, body, arms, and even in one case, a finger. The less severely injured, which included victims who fell or were pushed as they ran for safety, would wait for care in lieu of those who were fighting their gunshot wounds.

The other hospitals also felt the pain that was inflicted at the hands of Stephen Paddock. The University Medical Center of South Nevada treated 104 patients, four victims were treated at the UC Irvine Medical Center, and two others arrived at Southern California's Loma Linda University Medical Center. The Las Vegas sheriff would make an appeal to his community for blood donations; victims of the shooting desperately needed blood transfusions totaling 499 components during the first 24 hours of treatment.

Luckily, hundreds of individuals would comply with the sheriff's plea and lines to donate blood would stretch blocks of Las Vegas with individuals waiting more than six hours to give their blood to help those in need. The American Red Cross would report a 53% increase in blood donations two days after the mass shooting, and Las Vegas alone saw 800 units of blood donated. But, by Monday afternoon, 16 patients had already died, some on arrival and some after the medical professionals worked to save their lives and family members tried to find their loved ones.

At first, authorities had thought that Paddock had an accomplice who had helped him commit the horrible shooting spree. However, after the investigation was complete, the conclusion was made that there was no indication that anyone helped Paddock or was aware he was even planning his deadly mass shooting. There was skepticism as to how one man carried out the elaborate plan; however, it was clear Paddock acted on his own.

Once police and investigators finished their examination of Stephen Paddock and his deadly shooting, they would find 47 firearms in two of Paddock's houses and his hotel suite, all bought legally throughout Nevada, Utah, California, and Texas. There were also indications that Paddock didn't suddenly snap; instead, he had been planning a mass shooting for quite a while and was very calculated in his actions leading up to the massacre. Stephen Paddock premeditated the mass shooting and, in all accounts, wanted to take as many lives as possible. For example, during the year leading up to the shooting, Paddock had searched for the biggest open-air concert venues in the United States as well as the crowds along Santa Monica beach. He was more than likely trying to find the biggest number of carnage for his horrible plan.

It would be an understatement to say Stephen Paddock's family was shocked when they heard the news that he was behind the worst mass shooting in America's history. Eric Paddock explained his brother as just a normal guy and said "Mars just fell into the Earth...We're completely dumbfounded." Eric also wondered if he could have stopped his brother, a guilt he said he would carry with him for the rest of his life. As Eric tearfully stated, "Had I called him back instead of texting, would I have heard something in his voice? Would he have given up something? I don't know. I can't say."

And his brother, Bruce? He had not spoken to Stephen in around 10 years and only knew him as a law-abiding citizen who owned apartment buildings mostly. But, after he heard the massacre that was at the hands of his brother, Bruce stated that "I don't know how he could stoop to this low point, hurting someone else." Even Stephen's lawyer, Martin J. Kravitz, who was the lead attorney in Paddock's suit against the Cosmopolitan Hotel in 2012, called him bizarre, but not angry or a person that would have stood out in this type of situation.

There are questions about how Stephen Paddock was able to shoot into the crowd for nearly 10 minutes before law enforcement officials arrived at his hotel room to find him dead. Paddock had even shot security guard Jesus Campos six minutes before then opening fire on the country music crowd, yet police were not able to locate his exact location sooner. And, at first authorities had credited Campos for stopping the shooting, but it was later found that he was shot before the mass shooting had even started; Paddock fired 200 rounds into the hallway at 9:59 p.m. and officers did not find the wounded Campos until 10:18 p.m. This was when the security guard had directed the officers to Paddock's suite, but at that point Paddock had already stopped his massacre. There were also questions as to why, upon finding a security guard wounded by a gun shot, the officers did not immediately break into Paddock's hotel room. No one knows why Paddock stopped attacking the crowd of 22,000, although there were suspicions that the gunman had seen the security guard on his spy cameras and was ready to figure out an escape. Even though Campos was shot in the leg by Paddock, he still helped police clear other guests from the 32nd floor of the Mandalay Bay Hotel and Casino and was considered by many law enforcement officials to be a hero that fateful night.

All the ammunition and guns found at the scene illustrated that the casualties could have been even worse if Paddock had not seen anyone coming down the hallway. Among other things, authorities found approximately 4,000 unused rounds in Paddock's suite, which would have been much more than the 1,100 used to kill 58 and injure hundreds. He had a huge area in which to kill so many – literally multiple football fields' worth – and there is no question that if more bullets were shot, more fatalities would have been endured. Stephen Paddock did not need to aim at specific people; instead, he could just aim into the crowd knowing he would hit multiple victims.

THE GUNS USED
SPARK A NEW GUN DEBATE

W hen police finally confronted Stephen Paddock, he was dead with a self-inflicted gunshot wound to the head. Investigators found 23 guns in the room, including some very expensive firearms: .223-caliber AR-15-type rifles, .308-caliber AR-10-type rifles, a .308 caliber Ruger American bolt-action rifle, and a .38-caliber Smith and Wesson Model 342 revolver. A weapon that was identified as an AK-47-type rifle was equipped with a stand, which would steady the weapon while also improving its accuracy. In addition, a Colt AR-15, the same gun used by Aurora movie theatre mass shooter James Holmes and San Bernardino mass shooter Omar Mateen, was found. This type of firearm is the most popular rifle in the country, however, with an estimated eight million currently in American homes.

All of the guns found were expensive – from $5,000 to $10,000 each – and Paddock also had bipods in which to rest the rifles and steady his shooting, high-tech telescopic sights for accuracy, military grade .223 caliber ammunition, and special, high-capacity magazines that held up to 100 cartridges each. To put things in perspective, the standard United States infantry solder's magazine only holds 30 rounds. However, Nevada has no laws that limit ammunition magazine capacities.

Two of Paddock's semiautomatic rifles were equipped with medium-magnification scopes and two-legged supports. These tools should have helped him target specific people in the crowd. In addition, 12 of the rifles were fitted with bump-stock devices, which were legal and inexpensive ways to turn semi-automatic weapons into rapid-fire weapons to mimic fully automatic weapons. Since these guns fired like machine guns, they would explain how he was able to overwhelm the concert crowd of 22,000 with such devastation. Paddock may have had semiautomatic rifles, which fire a single round when the user pulls the trigger. However, when outfitted with bump-stock devices, the firing is much faster, similar to a fully automatic weapon. That way, Paddock was able to fire round after round, dozens of rounds in seconds, with simply one single pull of his finger. Since Paddock was said to have fired on the crowd for between nine and 11 minutes, in about a dozen bursts, this alone made the devastation that much more disastrous. Police who investigated the case also found a blue plastic hose in Paddock's hotel room, which had a fan on one end and a snorkel mouthpiece on the other end.

A bump stock basically helps the rifle slide a short distance back and forth so that it harnesses the recoil energy of each shot. What does that mean to a semi-automatic rifle? It literally "bumps" quickly between the shoulder and finger in order to create the action of repetition – the trigger pulls without the user having to move his or her finger trigger for each shot.

The weapons were purchased in Nevada, Utah, California, and Texas, and some of the ammunition was purchased under a different name. At first, this led investigators to believe Paddock had an accomplice, but this assumption was later debunked and they knew he had acted alone. After hours upon hours of review of surveillance video from the Mandalay Bay Hotel and

Casino, investigators were confident that there was not another shooter in the hotel room and Stephen Paddock had acted alone.

An unemployed chef, during a jailhouse interview at Clark County Detention Center where he was serving time on a possession charge (not related to guns, however), also claimed that he had offered to sell Paddock $40 schematics for automatic firearms. Paddock responded to his online ad that was selling the schematics, which showed how someone could transform a semi-automatic rifle into an automatic weapon. The two men had met in front of a Las Vegas sporting goods shot and he said Paddock had offered him $500 to make numerous AR-15s that could be converted from a semi-automatic weapon to an automatic weapon. However, the man turned down the offer, not wanting to spend time in a federal prison.

He also claimed that Paddock had spewed anti-government conspiracies, including ones about the Federal Emergency Management Agency's handling of Hurricane Katrina (claiming it was a slippery slope for federal law enforcement to start taking guns) and other right-wing injustices, such as the Wage and Ruby Ridge standoffs. He claimed that Paddock ranted about the government's plot to confiscate guns and even said Americans needed to wake up and arm themselves. Paddock supposedly had told him that, "Somebody has to wake up the American public and get them to arm themselves...Sometimes sacrifices have to be made." Although the man described Paddock as "fanatical," he also explained that he figured he was "another internet nut, you know, watching too much of it and believing too much of it."

How did Stephen Paddock smuggle in so many large weapons without anyone working at the Mandalay Bay Las Vegas Hotel noticing? In the days leading up to the shooting, Paddock would travel back to his home in Mesquite, Nevada, and then, with help from the hotel's bellmen, continue to bring suitcases into his hotel room at the Mandalay Bay. In total, Paddock brought five suitcases to his room on September 25th, seven on the 26th, two on the 28th, six on the 30th, and two more on the fateful day of October 1st. Police believe he used at least 10 suitcases four days earlier to sneak the weapons into the room, which he had actually checked in using his girlfriend, Marliou Dandy's, identification. Paddock even had access to the hotel's service elevator and used it in the days leading up to the mass shooting. Officers also reported that Paddock used Dandy's slot machine card to gamble with during his stay leading up to the massacre.

Vigils to honor the victims of the shooting were held in Reno, Las Vegas, and at the University of Nevada's Las Vegas campus. Another vigil was held on the corner of Sahara and Las Vegas Boulevard. Hundreds of people would take part in a candlelight memorial for Las Vegas police officer and Army veteran Charleston Hartfield, who was described as a father, joker, and big-hearted colleague. Even the expansion Vegas Golden Knights of the National Hockey League held a tribute to the victims and honored the response personnel who bravely helped the victims before their inaugural home game on October 10, 2017.

However, tragedy and violence would hit one of the survivors of the Las Vegas shooting a little more than a year later. On November 7, 2018, a mass shooting was committed by a 28-year-old United States Marine Corps veteran, David Long, at a country western bar called the Borderline Bar and Grill. The bar was mostly frequented by college students from four schools: Pepperdine University, California Lutheran University, California State University Channel Islands, and Moorpark College. However, some of the attendees on that night had survived Stephen Paddock's terror a little more than a year before. One survivor had said there may have been around 60 patrons at the Borderline Bar and Grill who had survived the 2017 Las Vegas shooting.

David Long had legally purchased a .45-caliber Glock 21 semi-automatic pistol, but also had seven banned high-capacity magazines for his mass shooting. Long killed nine men and three women – seven were college students, one was a recent graduate, along with four others – 54-year-old Ventura County Sheriff's Sergeant Ron Helus, who had arrived at the scene; a 48-year-old bouncer at the bar; a 33-year-old Marine Corps veteran; and a 27-year-old Navy veteran who had miraculously survived the Las Vegas shooting at the Route 91 Harvest Festival. This man's mother – a woman who watched her son survive one mass shooting only to be killed in another – would end up calling for more gun control legislation.

THE FUTURE OF GUNS IN AMERICA

Stephen Paddock was very prepared and, with his arsenal of firearms, ammunition, and modifications, made firing into a crowd that was around 500 yards away, equal to several football fields, not difficult to inflict mass bloodshed. After Paddock's mass shooting in Las Vegas, the Eastside Cannery Casino Gun Show that was supposed to be held in Las Vegas was cancelled, yet the sales of bump stocks spiked as gun advocates feared tighter gun regulations would follow the massacre. This is not surprising, as sales for firearms and accessories usually spike after a high-profile shooting takes place. The stock prices of firearms manufacturers also rose the day after Paddock's mass shooting, which has also happened after similar events in United States history. Yet, before Paddock's massacre, bump stocks were a relatively unknown device that was not widely sold in the United States. However, this changed after the Las Vegas mass shooting. For example, the owner of a Stockbridge, Georgia, shop called Ed's Public Safety said he would have been surprised if he sold two bump stocks in the past 10 years. After the shooting, he found it hard to find any available.

This came as a surprise to the actual inventor of the bump stock, Bill Akins, because he never made any money off his own creation. Atkins had come up with his idea in 1996 after watching a documentary about World War II. He saw barrels on Japanese warplanes that slid back and forth with each recoil and deliberated about designing a similar device for a semi-automatic rifle. This device would turn a firearm that fires once per trigger into a weapon capable of shooting hundreds of rounds per minute.

Atkins partnered with a firearms industry businessman and put his savings into his project called the "Akins Accelerator." He even put up his own property as collateral for a loan in order to start his business. At first, it was considered legal by the Bureau of Alcohol, Tobacco, Firearms and Explosives, but the ATF then banned the device in 2005. This is when another company, Slide Fire Solutions, made its own version of the bump stock that was approved by the ATF. Slide Fire's Facebook page even shows videos of individuals using their product, with one man firing off 58 rounds in only 12 seconds to celebrate his 58th birthday.

Atkins would transfer his own patent to the company FosTecH Outdoors and would then battle over patent infringement before settling in 2012. Although Atkins had tried for years to profit from his idea with his former business partner, a rival competitor, and even with the United States government, he was thwarted every time.

The government gave its official seal of approval for bump stocks in 2010, and they were thought to be helpful for people with disabilities to shoot a gun. However, they are now known for their capabilities of making a semi-automatic rifle nearly identical to a fully automatic weapon by allowing the shooter to release a whole magazine in only seconds. However, using a bump stock alone does not make the weapon that much more deadly; although it does allow a person to fire bullets more quickly, it really depends on what ammunition is used that makes the weapon that much more lethal.

These devices were normally legal and allowed a modified rifle to hold between 60 and 100 rounds. These devices also set off a new round of calls by Democratic lawmakers to pass more gun regulations, something Atkins has disagreed with. Although he did express his sorrow and condolences for the victims of the Las Vegas shooting, he also defends his stance that his devices are protected under the United States Constitution's right to bear arms under the Second Amendment.

The high-capacity magazines used by Paddock would also sell out after he used them to shoot more than 500 people in Las Vegas. The magazines, which hold up to 100 cartridges, would also sell out on at least three websites days after Paddock's massacre. The company that made the magazines that Paddock used, SureFire, sold out of both their $149 60-round magazine and $189 100-round magazine. Although this was the company that manufactured the high-capacity magazines used by Paddock, two other sites – BigArmory.com and GunmagWarehouse.com – were also sold out of the items. However, the investment company, Goldman Sachs, which invested in SureFire in 2007 and owned a 15% stake in the company (valued at around $11 million), would end up cutting its ties with the manufacturer after the mass shooting.

Modifications like bump stocks had not been considered to be making a gun into a machine gun, which is only legal if it was made before May 1986 and also registered with the federal government. They also did not qualify as an automatic weapon, which is also highly regulated by the United States. In all accounts, bump stocks were commonly seen at gun shows, although the term bump stock was not really known to the general public until Stephen Paddock used them to massacre nearly 60 innocent victims. And, police had said that the murder toll could have been even higher if Paddock had used more of the weapons they had found in his hotel room.

Although Atkins and others would defend the Second Amendment, this time, Democratic lawmakers and their Republican counterparts, including the Republican president of the United States, were willing to listen to possible gun law reform. When Donald Trump had campaigned for president against Hillary Clinton, he defended the Second Amendment against Clinton's agenda to strengthen and tighten gun laws. In fact, President Trump, once in office, worked with his Republican-controlled Congress to reverse a rule that the Obama administration had implemented after the Virginia Tech shooting, in which 32 people were killed on April 16, 2007 after gunman, Seung-Hui Cho, began shooting at the school. Cho was a 23-year-old senior who was diagnosed with multiple mental issues over the years. The gunman entered a classroom building, chained and locked many of the main doors to impede anyone's chances of escape, and left 27 students and five faculty members dead. Cho was armed with a 9-millimeter handgun, a 22-caliber handgun, and hundreds of rounds of ammunition – all firearms bought legally.

Two days later, NBC News received a package of materials sent by Cho, which showed him in photos brandishing a gun and a video showing him ranting about wealthy brats, among other things. During the final days of the Obama administration, a law was passed to allow the Social Security Administration to provide information to the gun background check system of individuals who had severe mental disabilities, such as Cho. Although President Trump would then reverse this rule finalized by the Obama administration and run as a defendant of the Second Amendment, he surprised many conservatives and gun owners when he voiced his concern of bump stocks.

However, the Democratic and Republican parties would clash on how to review gun laws without politicizing the worst mass shooting in the United States. For example, Sen. John Thune, the third-ranking Republican in the Senate at that time, did think the legislators should look at how these types of conversion kits make guns more deadly. However, he also noted that little change could be accomplished through legislation.

Vice President Mike Pence visited Las Vegas to offer his consolation and support, joining Las Vegas Mayor Carolyn Goodman, who called Paddock a "crazed lunatic full of hate" and other local leaders who were still reeling from the grief of what happened in their city in a citywide "unity prayer walk" that was held in honor of the mass shooting victims. When President Donald Trump visited Las Vegas days after the massive shooting, he called Stephen Paddock "a sick man, a demented man, lot of problems, I guess. We're looking into him very, very seriously." The president's Air Force 1 landed at McCarran International Airport at 9:37 a.m. on Wednesday, October 4, 2017, and along with his wife, first lady Melania Trump, planned to visit medical staff, patients, first responders, and the civilians who did heroic acts during the mass shooting. Just the day before he had visited victims of Hurricane Maria in Puerto Rico.

The first couple visited doctors and patients at the University Medical Center, the Level 1 trauma center that treated more than 100 victims after the mass shooting. The president voiced how proud it makes one to be an American when he or she sees the job the medical professionals had done to help the victims. The president also praised the police for the incredible job he said they did to responding to the mass shooting and stopping the gunfire. The president and first lady visited the Las Vegas Metropolitan Police Department during their time in Las Vegas.

During the National Clean Energy Summit at the Bellagio Resort and Casino, about a mile from the Mandalay Bay on the Las Vegas' strip, attendees also remembered the victims and the mass shooting. Former Vice President Al Gore, who was slated to give the keynote address, noted how the tragedy wounded everyone deeply but also brought everyone together – he said the entire country was grieving for Las Vegas.

President Trump issued a proclamation that ordered flags to be flown at half-staff until October 6, 2017. He also said something not usually uttered by Republican politicians – he hinted that there would be some sort of discussion about gun legislation. Now, it was not surprising that Democrats came out against guns after the mass shooting, as firearms and devices are usually scrutinized by Democratic lawmakers and gun-control advocates after such a horrific event. What was even more surprising was that some top Republican lawmakers agreed with him. There were some pro-gun Republican lawmakers and even the powerful gun lobby, the National Rifle Association, who suggested they would support an evaluation and assessment of bump stocks.

Sen. Diane Feinstein, a California Democrat, has tried to ban bump stocks for years, and after the Las Vegas shooting she renewed this call for action. Yet, after the massacre, Congressional Democrats called upon their Republican counterparts to establish a special committee to investigate gun violence in America. Democratic Sen. Chris Murphy of Connecticut, a leading gun-control proponent, voiced that he believed it was time for Congress to act and called mass shootings an "epidemic" in America. And, the House Minority Leader Democrat from California, Nancy Pelosi, issued a powerful decree: "Today, our nation woke up to news of the worst mass shooting in our history, claiming the lives of at least 58 innocent men and women in Las Vegas. Nearly 12,000 Americans have been killed by guns in 273 mass shootings in 2017 – one for each day of the year." Representative Pelosi turned to her Republican counterpart, House Speaker Paul Ryan from Wisconsin, to develop a committee on gun violence to begin reviewing what she and other Democrats would call common sense gun legislation.

To the surprise of gun enthusiasts, some top Republicans in the United States Congress acknowledged that they would be open to banning bump-stock devices. For example, Sen. John Cornyn, the number two Republican in the Senate from Texas, admitted that he did not understand the use of bump stocks and they should explore them more to see if Congress needs to take action. Another Republican Texas lawmaker, Rep. Bill Flores, went a step further and called for an outright ban on bump-stock conversion devices. For a party who for decades had rejected nearly any form of gun restrictions or regulations, the GOP began to raise questions about bump stock devices and their legality under federal law.

The National Rifle Association even endorsed tighter restrictions on the bump stock devices, a surprise move for the association that usually does not allow any chipping away at Second Amendment rights. Although the group did not say whether bump stocks should be outlawed entirely, an NRA spokesperson did state that the group would immediately review whether the devices complied with federal law. The group also noted that, if the devices do indeed allow semi-automatic rifles to function like fully automatic rifles, they may need more regulations than they are currently subject to under the existing law.

Probably the most controversial legislation that came out of the Las Vegas shooting was the "Keep Americans Safe Act." This bill, H.R. 1186, was introduced by Rep. Ted Deutch, a Democrat from Florida who sits on the Judiciary Committee. Eighteen Democratic United States Senators introduced this bill following the mass shooting in order to ban gun magazines that hold more than 10 rounds of ammunition. More specifically, the bill would prohibit the importation, sales, manufacturing, transferring, or possession of these magazines for civilian use. Anyone who already owed this style of ammunition would be grandfathered in under the bill, and law enforcement officials, active or retired, along with those using them to secure nuclear materials would be allowed to still have access to magazines that hold more than 10 rounds of ammunition. However, for everyone else, they would now be illegal under H.R. 1186.

The bill did not have any Republican co-sponsors but was approved by the House Judiciary Committee in September 2019. Other Democratic-led committee plans for gun control, such as more stringent background checks and "red flag" laws, would need bipartisan support with the Republican-controlled Senate. Judiciary Chairman Jerrold Nadler, a Democrat from New York, would call on his Senate associates and state to them that, ""I call on my Senate colleagues to join us in this effort by swiftly passing gun safety bills the House has already passed and also by acting on the additional bills we will be considering."

The red flag laws did have some Republican support; that is, H.R. 1236, the Extreme Risk Protection Order of 2019, had 159 sponsors – 157 Democrats and two Republicans, Brian Fitzpatrick of Pennsylvania and Christopher Smith of New Jersey. Rep. Smith had added his name to the bill after two more mass shooting occurred, one in El Paso, Texas, and one in, Dayton, Ohio. On August 3, 2019, Patrick Crusius, a 21-year-old from Allen, Texas, shot and killed 23 people and injured 23 others at a Walmart in El Paso, Texas. Then one day later, on August 4, 2019, a 24-year-old man named Connor Stephen Betts shot and killed nine people and wounded 17 more individuals near the entrance of the Ned Peppers Bar.

This bill was introduced by Rep. Salud Carbajal, a Democrat from California, on the anniversary of the Marjory Stoneman Douglas High School shooting in Parkland, Florida, when a gunman opened fire at the school and killed 17 people. Commonly known as the "red flag" law, this bill would allow law enforcement to remove firearms from the homes of individuals who may be believed to be an imminent threat to either themselves or others.

Finally, H.R. 2708, entitled the Disarm Hate Act, was also introduced by Rep. David Cicilline, Democrat from Rhode Island and a member of the Judiciary. This legislation had 129 co-sponsors – all Democrats – and would add anyone who was convicted of a misdemeanor hate crime to the list of those who are barred from owning firearms. Currently, there are nine categories of individuals who are prohibited from owning firearms under the Gun Control Act besides those under 18 years of age (who cannot own handguns): anyone indicted for or convicted of a felony that is punishable by more than one year in prison; fugitives from justice; unlawful users or those addicted to controlled substances; those who are declared as mental defectives by a court or have been committed to a mental institution; illegal aliens or aliens admitted to the United States under a nonimmigrant visa; anyone who was dishonorably discharged from the Armed Forces; anyone who has had their United States citizenship renounced; those who were convicted of domestic violence, a misdemeanor crime; and individuals subject to certain types of restraining orders. This new bill would add those convicted of misdemeanor hate crimes to this long list and would be enforced through background checks.

Regarding background checks, H.R. 1112, the Enhanced Background Checks Act, was introduced by the Majority Whip, Democrat James Clyburn of South Carolina, and was passed in the House with most Democrats voting in favor of the bill, but only three Republicans in support – Fitzpatrick, Smith, and Republican Peter King of New York. This bill is fighting to fill the loophole that allows the purchase of a gun if an individual is not flagged by a federal background check within three business days by extending that window to 10 business days. This loophole was allegedly used by white supremacist and mass murderer Dylan Roof, who perpetrated the Charleston church shooting on June 17, 2015 in South Carolina. Roof was able to purchase a Glock 41.45-caliber handgun and used it to kill nine people at the predominately black church even those his previous drug conviction should have made him ineligible under the Gun Control Act. An error in the FBI background check process allowed him to purchase the firearm. Once Roof was captured by law enforcement, he admitted that he intentionally committed the mass murders to ignite a race war.

BUMP STOCKS ARE OFFICIALLY BANNED IN THE UNITED STATES

The Las Vegas shooting also brought bump-stock devices into the spotlight in the media, in the legislature, and in the minds of gun owners and Second Amendment activists. As discussed, Stephen Paddock had enhanced 12 of his semi-automatic rifles with these bump-stock devices so that they would shoot similarly to fully automatic rifles. Fully automatic weapons, which fire multiple rounds of ammunition with just a single pull of the trigger, are strictly regulated under the United States law, are taxed, and are even tracked. Because of the expense of purchasing, taxing, and regulating this type of weapon, they are usually considered more of a collector's items for those who can afford them, not a weapon to be used in a crime. Although fully automatic weapons were banned in the United States in 1986, there have been permissible attachments, such as bump-stocks, that allow guns to fire like fully automatic rifles.

Unlike a semi-automatic rifle, which requires the user to pull the trigger after firing each round, a modified bump stock only requires one pull and then the device's spring mechanism pulls the trigger repeatedly. Therefore, one single pull on a modified semi-automatic rifle can allow an entire magazine to be continuously unloaded. This device essentially turns a semi-automatic rifle, which is legal in the United States, into an outlawed fully automatic weapon. Although it was rumored that these devices were originally created to help disabled gun owners, the term bump stock was rarely known before Paddock's massacre, but after the horrific event sales of the modification device spiked so much that, in many cases, bump stocks began selling out at gun stores.

Semi-automatic weapons that have been modified to work similarly to fully automatic weapons have long been a political fight, with Democrats and gun-control advocates fighting for them to be banned. However, gun-rights advocates have also fought on this issue, remarking that semi-automatic weapons are no more dangerous than semi-automatic hunting rifles (which are rarely a political target by Democrats). In addition, some researchers have mentioned that most gun murders are committed with handguns, not semi-automatic weapons.

Paddock also used another controversial item in the minds of some lawmakers and advocates: large capacity ammunition magazines. These give users the ability to fire dozens of rounds of ammunition without having to reload. When the 1994 federal assault weapons ban came about under President Bill Clinton, Congress limited the production and sale of certain kinds of semi-automatic weapons and high-capacity ammunition magazines. This ban, however, expired in 2004 and, under President George W. Bush, was not renewed. Some states, such as California, have their own assault weapon bans and limits on magazines in place.

Many gun enthusiasts heard the legislative outcry for tougher gun controls that could block the ownership of certain weapons, such as ones that can be legally modified to work as a fully functioning assault rifle. There were also specific calls to prohibit the sales of bump stocks in particular, which only fueled the sales of the devices before any action may have been taken by politicians. Some stores, such as Walmart and Cabela's (two of the largest gun and gun accessory retailers in the United States), voluntarily stopped selling bump-stock devices. Walmart had said they pulled the devices because they determined they violated their prohibited items policy and never should have been sold on their site in the first place. However, smaller gun retailers continued to sell out of the devices in the wake of the shooting and possible legislation.

On November 6, 2017, Massachusetts became the first state to ban the sale, possession, or use of bump stock devices. One year after the shooting, 11 states would ban bump stocks, and more than a dozen additional states and cities would consider the ban. Then, nearly a year later, in December 2018, the United States Justice Department and acting United States Attorney General Matthew Whitaker signed a regulation to officially ban bump stocks in the United States. This regulation went into effect in March 2019 and requires any current owner of a bump stock to either surrender or destroy the devices.

IN CONCLUSION...

The investigation of the Las Vegas shooting would last more than a year, yet there would still be questions unanswered. When the FBI would finally close its investigation on the Las Vegas mass shooting that killed more than any other mass shooting in United States history, an FBI Behavioral Analysis Unit would conclude that they could not find a single or clear motive for what Stephen Paddock had done. They did presume that he was in financial trouble and had some difficulties handling his age, but these factors still did not help authorities determine a specific motive for Paddock's reign of terror on so many innocent victims.

In most mass shootings, a motive is clear, whether it is left in a note, a social media post, or even a phone call made by the killer. This was not the case with Stephen Paddock. Days after the deadliest mass shooting in America's history, investigators still could not find the motive of Stephen Paddock. Investigators would chase thousands of leads, review 22,000 hours of video from hotel cameras, private cameras, and police body cameras, evaluate 252,000 images, and around one-thousand legal processes. Hundreds of interviews would be completed to try to put the puzzle together as to why Stephen Paddock would commit such a horrific crime. They would examine everything from Paddock's political leanings and possible radicalization, to his finances and social circles. In the end, it seemed the coldest-blooded killer in American history was simply a retired accountant, real estate investor, and self-made millionaire who now spent his time gambling in front of video poker machines. Certainly not the portrait of a cold-blooded killer, but he was one, nonetheless.

It was determined that Paddock had acted alone, as law enforcement officials would be confident that he was the only shooter. According to investigators, no one else entered Paddock's hotel room on the 32nd floor prior to the shooting. However, the motive was always unclear, and as time went on, this did not change. This aspect was probably one of the most difficult realizations for the individuals whose loved ones' lives were taken away by the hands of Stephen Paddock. Finding out the motive of a killer can sometimes help bring a sense of closure to the survivors of a killer's mayhem and it can help form legislative policy to possibly stop a similar event. The survivors and loved ones who were inflicted by the Las Vegas mass shooting will never get this closure. The fact that the killings could have been random – find a place with a lot of people and shoot – make the lives lost that much more devastating. That being said, Stephen Paddock meticulously planned out his mass shooting – more than likely, he had a reason.

Legally, it is hard to say why Stephen Paddock murdered innocent concert goers, whether he had a motive, and if he is even considered a terrorist under the law. Under Nevada law, it seemed pretty clear that he would be considered a terrorist in that there were no severe mental problems found that could question is criminal intent. The law defines terrorism in the state as any event that "is intended to...cause great bodily harm or death to the general population." He did, indeed, terrorize the Las Vegas community and the loved ones whose family and friends lost their lives and were terrorized on that fateful day.

Did Paddock spur potential copycats? Soon after his massacre, the FBI warned law enforcement partners of a potential threat in New York City's famous tourist attraction Times Square. An Instagram user had posted the following: "I'm a Syrian refugee and I'm going to do something big in New York on Friday...I'm going to make the Las Vegas attack look small on Friday at Times Square." It is unclear whether this poster was inspired by Paddock's mass shooting, but the poster did specifically reference Las Vegas before comparing it to what the potential attacker was going to do in New York City. However, New York City never would have an attack and the FBI and New York City Police Department both deemed the threat as not credible after tracing the IP addresses associated with the Instagram post to South Africa.

The casualties inflicted by mass shootings have gone up since 1984. The numbers have risen as follows for the six deadliest mass shootings in the United States: 21 killed at the McDonalds in California; 23 killed at Lubys Cafeteria in Killeen, Texas, in 1991; 32 killed in 2007 at Virginia Tech; 27 killed at Sandy Hook Elementary in Connecticut in 2012; and the two most recent and deadly – 50 killed in 2016 at the Orlando, Florida, Pulse Nightclub and 58 killed by Stephen Paddock in Las Vegas. So, Paddock's massacre resulted in the most deaths by a mass shooter.

Gun laws have been modified after numerous mass shootings, and the same is slightly true after the Las Vegas massacre. After the 2007 Virginia Tech massacre, President George W. Bush signed into law a measure to expand the FBI's National Instant Criminal Background Check System. Then, his successor, President Barack Obama, continued to work on gun legislation. An unsuccessful bill was also introduced after a shooting in Tucson, Arizona, that left six dead and seriously wounded Rep. Gabrielle Giffords, a Democrat from Arizona. Although this bill, which strived to ban high-capacity ammunition magazines to a maximum of 10 rounds, failed in the Senate, Rep. Giffords would become a staple and leader in gun legislation reform.

After the mass shooting at Sandy Hook Elementary that killed 20 children and six adults, a law was also introduced which would have expanded background checks and limited the size of magazines. This law also failed by only a few votes in the Senate, 54-46. Congress did renew a federal ban that same year, however, on plastic firearms that could go undetected in X-ray machines or metal detectors. This would be the last major gun-related bill to be signed into law, as other mass shootings – San Bernardino and the Orlando Pulse nightclub – would not see compromise in the legislature. So, what is the state of gun laws today ever since Stephen Paddock reigned down terror on a group of 22,000 country music concertgoers?

In March 2019, bump stocks became officially illegal through a Trump administration ban. Anyone owning or selling bump stocks could now face up to 10 years in a federal prison and a fine of $250,000 per violation. In addition, this ban does not have a grandfather clause, which means anyone who previously owned bump stocks were required to either turn them into law enforcement authorities or destroy the equipment. This is because the new law classifies the devices as machine guns, which makes owning one a felony. Companies that produced the controversial piece of equipment rushed to sell them before having to turn over their inventory to the ATF. Some gun owners tried to fight the ban, but the Las Vegas shooting was a convincing reason for the legislature to hold solid on the new law.

Stephen Paddock was the son of a notorious bank robber, known to be quite unfriendly and cold, and was even seen as verbally insulting to his girlfriend. However, he was also a well-off real estate and businessman who took his girlfriend on cruises, lavish dinners, and gambled thousands upon thousands a night at various Las Vegas casinos. He was a 64-year-old man who lived an itinerant lifestyle, traveling from place to place while engaging in high-stakes gambling along the way. No one saw any red flags – there was no radical political affiliation, no strong interest in firearms, no history of violence, no mental-health issues beyond a fear of germs and some anxiety. There was no way anyone could have known that one man could have ruined the lives of so many.

Made in the USA
Las Vegas, NV
02 January 2022

39885601R10060